Stories THEY WILL REMEMBER

Rose D. Sloat
Darryl S. Doane

HRD Press, Inc. • Amherst • Massachusetts

Published by: Human Resource Development Press, Inc.
22 Amherst Road
Amherst, Massachusetts 01002
1-800-822-2801 (U.S. and Canada)
1-413-253-3488
1-413-253-3490 (fax)
www.hrdpress.com

Copyright © 2005 by Darryl S. Doane and Rose D. Sloat

ISBN 0-87425-870-7

All rights reserved. *It is a violation of the law* to reproduce, store in a retrieval system or transmit, in any form or by any means, electronic, mechanical, photocopying, recording or otherwise, any part of this publication without the prior written permission of the copyright owner.

Typeset by Wordstop Technologies (P) Ltd., Chennai, India

Editorial services provided by Sally Farnham

Cover design by Eileen Klockars

Cover photo by Joe Smithberger

Dedication

To my Father, Steve Doane, and to my Mother, Anne M. Doane
—Darryl S. Doane

To my Father, James E. DeAngelo, Sr., and my Mother, Lillian C. Hays
—Rose D. Sloat

Contents

Dedication iii
Introduction vii
The Stories and Their Applications 1
    The Two Monks 3
    Impersonating Someone Who Cares 7
    So Close to Victory 11
    Remember My Name 15
    What Do You Do? 19
    Shake and Step 23
    The Dance 27
    The Worst Day 31
    Always Remember Those Who Serve 37
    The Greatest Hurdler 41
    Message Received 45
    We Want Coffee 49
    The Hammer and the Fence 53
    The Obstacle in Our Path 59
    Catching Monkeys 63
    A Learning Experience 67
    The Pledge 71
    Getting Enough Air? 75
    Giving When It Counts 81
    Talk'n About Me, Weren't You? 85
    Our New Car 89
    Please, Sorry, Love, and Thanks 93

The Little Bitty Frying Pan 97
The Mariner 101
Building Bridges 105
Planes, Ships, and People 111
Dynamite 115
Rear View Mirror 119
Everything is Just Fine! 123
He's My Friend 127
Killer Statements 131
PIG! 135
Get Her the Oranges! 139
The Cook, the Carpenter, and the Engineer 143
Pandora's Box Revisited 147
You Can't Put It Back 151
Where are You Going? 155
The Game 159
The Teachers' Lounge 163
What is Your Story? 167

Authors' Personal Information 171

Introduction

If you've ever been preparing a talk or presentation and needed just that little extra something to get your message across in a meaningful way that would be remembered, this book is for you. Stories have been used as powerful learning tools for centuries: from the teachings of Aristotle and Socrates to the parables and teachings of Christ, to the many myths, yarns, and anecdotes of people like Abraham Lincoln, Will Rogers, and so many of our greatest motivational speakers. These are the master storytellers who realize the power that a good story wields in delivering its message and its ability to strengthen and renew a learning experience, a key concept, or a primary idea through its being remembered and retold.

In this book you will find a variety of such stories—stories we have gathered over the past thirty years from our own personal experiences, our travels, and the many thousands of individuals we have presented to and worked with over the years. We have discussed each story and its various applications to make it easier for you to select the appropriate story for your particular situation.

We believe that everyone has a meaningful story within them. To assist in bringing your story to the surface and encourage its telling and sharing, we have included guidelines for the development of your own personal stories.

Besides providing personal satisfaction, these tales can help build corporate culture as well as team, department, and company cohesiveness. On a personal level, our hope is that these stories will touch your heart and provide you with personal encouragement and positive growth.

This book was written with many individuals in mind—trainers, consultants, motivational speakers, CEOs, department heads, supervisors, managers, teachers, and anyone with a desire to leave a lasting impression through the use of a recognized, established, powerful tool—story telling. You will find that each section of this book has been divided for your convenience into the following areas:

- **Applications.** What is the "best fit" for this particular story? Suggestions are given followed by a bulleted list of **Three-Key Applications** for ease of use.
- **The Story.** The actual story is told in this section.
- **Other Insights.** This section contains a variety of questions, comments, ideas, and food for thought—items intended to spur your own creativity as you apply the story to your own situation or program.

Darryl S. Doane
Rose D. Sloat

The Stories and Their Applications

The Two Monks—Applications

This particular story has numerous applications including effectively dealing with change and letting go of a bad experience. Often when confronting change, we reflect on past experiences that are similar in nature, commonly referred to as resonance. When we carry these past feelings or "baggage" with us, they can present an obstacle that at times prevents us from clearly focusing on what is actually happening in the present and dealing effectively with it.

The story of the two monks reflects the emotions of holding on for too long to something that occurred in the past and how that inability to let go can take its toll. In this day of intense, fast-paced change, it's an excellent story that allows individuals to focus on transition—the personal, psychological, emotionalism attached to change that usually varies from person to person.

Three Key Applications

- Resonance
- Letting Go
- Dealing with Change

The Two Monks— The Story

Many years ago, there was a monastery in southern France. This particular order had very specific rules their members had to follow. One of the rules was that there was to be absolutely no talking until after dinner each evening. One of the other rules was that they were not allowed to look at or touch any woman.

Two of the members of the order, one an elder monk and the other much younger, were traveling by foot to visit a neighboring monastery. As the monks were making their way through the countryside, they came upon a river they had to cross. The river was wider than past encounters due to recent heavy rains and had a rather strong current. Right in front of the monks where they would be crossing was a woman struggling to cross with little success. The older monk went right up to the woman, picked her up in his arms, and carried her across the river. Upon arriving at the other bank, he set her down and immediately continued on his way.

The younger monk was shocked. He could not believe what he had just observed. He had also made his way across the river, following right behind the older monk. He wanted to speak out and confront his partner with what had just occurred, but he was not allowed to speak. Remember the rules: no talking until after dinner. So, all the rest of the day this was just eating him up inside, but he abided by the rule.

Finally, as the day wore on and with hardly any daylight left, they stopped and selected an area to spend the night. They gathered firewood, built a fire, and prepared their evening meal. After dinner, the younger monk wasted little time in confronting the older monk: "You picked up that woman!" he said. The older monk replied, "Yes, I did. I picked her up. I carried her across the river and set her down. You on the other hand have been carrying her all day long!"

Other Insights:

- What items have you been carrying too long?
- What do you need to put down and let go of so that you can continue to move forward with your life?
- Are the standards you follow so rigid that they allow for no flexibility when confronting an obstacle, goal, or challenge?
- Do you wear a mental straight jacket that confines your creativity and your growth?

Allow for flexibility when confronting an obstacle, goal, or challenge.

Impersonating Someone Who Cares—Applications

This story applies to behavior that reinforces our values and beliefs. Our outside (observable behavior) needs to match up with what is on the inside and must not be hypocritical of our real self. Living a lie or putting on a facade can be very deceiving not only to others, but to our self. Be careful not to impersonate someone who really cares. This story is about taking a good hard look at who we really are, reflecting on what we believe and value, and being certain that our behaviors mirror those inner feelings.

Three Key Applications

- Values
- Beliefs
- Behaviors

Impersonating Someone Who Cares—The Story

A young lady was on her way to the mall. As she drove down the road, she was anxious to begin her day off, meeting her friends and doing what she truly loved—shopping. As she approached an intersection, she came to a stop behind a car, which had also been caught by the red light. She was impatient and tapped her fingers on the steering wheel.

As the light turned to green, she prepared to move on, but something was wrong. The car in front of her was not moving. The man in the car seemed to be unaware that the light had changed. At first she simply uttered, "Come on, let's move it" and hit the top of her steering wheel. Two other cars went around them and on through the intersection, but the young lady had pulled so close to the car that she could not simply go around it. She honked her horn and began to shout as the passage of seconds seemed like an eternity and her patience was completely gone.

She began to yell out loud, cursing the man in the car, honking with continual duration, and lowering her window. She leaned her head out the window yelling and giving an obscene hand gesture to no avail. The car did not move, and the light was beginning to change again.

As the light turned yellow, the man, for whatever reason, seemed to come to life and at the last second moved on through the intersection leaving the young outraged lady trapped at the red light once again. She continued her now out-of-control tirade oblivious to the police car that had pulled up behind her. The officer had gotten out of his car and walked up to the young lady's car as she continued her outburst. The officer's tap on the top of the car startled her, and she stared in shock at the policeman who had seemed to suddenly appear. He asked her to step out of the car and place her hands on the vehicle. Then as she stood there stunned by what was happening, he had her place her hands behind her as he handcuffed her and led her to the police car.

She was driven to the police station and placed in a holding cell for over two hours. Another officer finally came in to the cell, opened the door, and led the young lady to a room where the arresting officer was also present. She was asked to sit down, and the officer who had brought her to the jail said to her, "It appears that I have mistakenly deterred you, and you will be allowed to leave. When I pulled up behind you while you were still ranting and raving, I noticed the stickers on the back of the car. One read, 'Do unto others as you would have them do unto you,' while another said, 'Practice random acts of kindness,' while another stated, 'Respect, kindness and caring count!'" "Quite frankly ma'am," the officer stated, "I thought you had stolen the car."

Be careful not to be accidentally mistaken for someone who cares!

Other Insights:

Our actions often speak much louder than our words. Our outward actions should truly reflect what we believe inside. Is your behavior consistent with your beliefs and values?

Don't get caught impersonating someone who cares.

So Close to Victory—Applications

Every time we tell this story, we cannot help but think about what it truly means to be a professional.

This story focuses on the need to maintain an awareness of the environment we are operating in and the rules that we must adhere to in order to properly function at our best. In today's world, being a true professional means many things. This is an excellent introductory or concluding statement with regard to professionalism, and this story stimulates further thought and discussion on the topic of what it means to be a professional.

Three Key Applications

- Know the Rules
- Recognize Opportunities
- Take Action

So Close to Victory—
The Story

We were speaking with a football coach from a high school out West. He shared the following story with us:

His high school team had not won a single game in almost three full seasons. It was the final game of the third season. There were seven seconds left in the game, and they were one field goal (three points) ahead as the game was drawing to a close. To top it off, they had possession of the ball. The coach and his players were beside themselves to finally realize that the long-awaited victory was within their grasp. The coach called his players over to huddle around him. "Gentlemen," he said, "I want you to forget about the past seasons and the defeat we have experienced. Tonight is our Super Bowl. We are finally about to experience victory. This one is ours! Every one of the fans is standing and they are about to count down the clock with us. Now, all you have to do is go out there, take the snap, and this is our moment."

That was all the coach said as his team ran out, huddled, and took their position on the field. The quarterback took the snap and fell back. Seven, six, five…the clock counted down with the fans shouting the count down out loud. Again, every time this story is told, we cannot help but think of professionalism and what it means to be a professional. Four, three, two…the official clock continued to count down. Now the quarterback, being caught up in the excitement of the moment with only two seconds left and experiencing that thrill of apparent victory after all those losses, took the ball and, with both hands around it, threw it into the air with a big yell. Again, whenever this story is told, we cannot help but think about what it means to be a professional. One thing that being a professional means is knowing the rules of the game you are playing. A player on the other team observed what had happened. He knew the rules of the game. He was aware that the ball was just thrown straight up into the air and was very much a live ball in a game that was not yet over.

Being a professional also means having the ability to recognize opportunities. That ball was identified by this same player as an opportunity. Being a professional means not just recognizing opportunities, but knowing when it is the appropriate moment to take action. The player on the opposing team knew the rules. He recognized the opportunity, and he gave himself permission to take action. He ran under the ball as it plummeted to earth, caught it on the run, and never looked back until he crossed the goal line and was in the end zone. Touchdown!

By the way, we were talking to the ex-head coach of that team. He had lost again—three complete seasons without a victory. However, he was not the one we felt so sorry for. It was that young quarterback who, in his enthusiasm, literally threw the victory that was so close right out of his grasp. He was going to have to live with that for the rest of his life.

Being a professional can mean so many things.

Other Insights:

What does being a professional mean to you?

What attributes do you feel an individual must possess to truly be a professional?

Know the rules of the game you are playing. Recognize opportunities and give yourself permission to take action.

Remember My Name—Applications

We need to treat everyone with the same respect and dignity with which we would like to be treated. Every single person within your organization is important and in some way makes a significant contribution. Be certain not to take anyone for granted or to be condescending to anyone within your company.

Three Key Applications

- Applying the Golden Rule
- Treating Every Person Equally
- Recognizing All Contributors

Remember My Name— The Story

During my second month of college, one of my professors gave a pop quiz. I was a conscientious student and had breezed through the questions until I read the last one, "What is the first name of the woman who cleans the school?"

Surely this was some kind of joke. I had seen the cleaning woman several times. She was tall, dark haired, and in her 50s, but how would I know her name? I handed in my paper, leaving the last question blank.

Just before class ended, one student asked if the last question would count toward our quiz grade. "Absolutely," said the professor. "In your careers, you will meet many people. All are significant. They deserve your attention and care, even if all you do is smile and say 'hello.'"

I've never forgotten that lesson. I also learned her name was Dorothy.

—Anonymous

Other Insights:

Remember the "Golden Rule," and we don't mean "He who has the gold makes the rules," but rather "Do unto others as you would have them do unto you."

Are there "invisible people" within your organization—those who quietly do their jobs day in and day out with little or no recognition? Pay attention to those people for they, in their own way, contribute to the success of your organization. Every single position is significant and adds to the success of the entire company.

Every single member of your organization contributes in some way to the success of your organization.

What Do You Do?— Applications

We all at times need to take a step back and take stock in ourselves. This story asks the listeners to take a sincere, reflective look at what they do—what they do as professionals in whatever their positions or areas of concentration might be. This can be on an individual, a small group, or a team basis. It calls on individuals to think of the impact they have on others as a result of their actions and behaviors. We are each inescapably responsible for our actions and the consequences of those actions whether they are positive or negative.

Three Key Applications

- Self-reflection
- Being a Professional
- Having an Awareness of Our Actions and Behaviors

What Do You Do?— The Story

A few years ago, we were involved in a national leadership conference. This conference included a cross section of participants from high schools, colleges, and adult corporate arenas. We were pleased to be part of an accomplished group of presenters. As we waited back stage for the opening ceremonies and introductions to commence, we noticed a young man in a wheelchair. He was rather disfigured from injuries or physical mishaps that had been brought upon him. He also had a difficult time with his speech and being understood. As we walked closer to this young man, he looked up at us, and with apparent effort as a result of his afflictions, he said, "Hi, my name is Michael. What do you do?" We looked at Michael and said, "Hi, Michael. We are (insert names here), and we're here to present part of the program this morning." Michael looked directly at us and said, "Well, my name is Michael, and I'm a singer." He then repeated, "What do you do?" As he finished these words, another individual grasped the handles of Michael's wheelchair and directed him out to the center of the stage.

We couldn't help but wonder what this young man was going to do. Michael was taken out to center stage and positioned by a microphone that had been placed specifically for him. The spotlight was focused on Michael, and the participants, who numbered over seven hundred, grew silent. Then from the voice of this young man came the most beautiful rendition of *The Star Spangled Banner* we had ever heard. It was amazing and flawless. When Michael was singing, it was perfect, and after he was done, the audience responded with a standing ovation that lasted several minutes. The applause diminished, and once again the individual who had assisted Michael appeared to bring him off stage. As Michael approached us, he looked directly at us and reiterated, "I'm Michael and I'm a singer. What do you do?" Those words—what do you do—have stayed with us.

Similar to Michael's story above is a story related to 9/11. We were watching TV with shocked disbelief as the horrors of that tragic day unfolded before us. A fireman had just appeared from the rubble with white ghostly soot enveloping his entire body. He stepped forward with a news crew following his every move. He took his hat off, removed what appeared to be an oxygen tank and mask, and unbuttoned his coat while taking a deep breath. You could see he was just trying to regain his composure, his strength, and his understanding. Someone handed him a bottle of water, and after a brief sip, he began to button up his coat. He then put on his tank, mask, hat, and other tools of his trade. The reporter who had been watching his every move while the camera was directly focused on the fireman said, "You're not going back in there, are you?" The fireman, without hesitation, looked directly at the camera and exclaimed, "Of course, I am. That's what I do." He then proceeded back into the inferno.

What do you do? Those words stayed with us. As a professional, what do you do? What a perfect time to concentrate and reflect on this.

Other Insights:

The average professional football player spends between 40 and 60 hours in practice for each one hour on the field. How much time do you spend practicing your chosen profession? How much time do you spend practicing *what you do?*

It was Coach Vince Lombardi who said, "Practice doesn't make perfect. It's perfect practice that makes perfect."

Remember the joke by the late Henny Youngman? It went something like this: He was standing on a street corner in New York City when a taxi pulled up. Henny motioned to the driver who lowered his window. "Could you tell me how to get to Carnegie Hall?" asked Henny. "Sure I can," the driver replied. "Practice, practice, practice." Isn't it the truth? We need to practice our profession and constantly give ourselves permission to improve. As professionals, we need to do whatever is right, necessary, proper, and just. *What do you do?*

What are you going to do to be certain that your professionalism comes to the surface to be seen, heard, or displayed? Often the one critical factor that differentiates our company from the rest of the pack (the competition) is our professionalism—our service. *What do you do?*

How much time do you spend practicing to be the professional that you are? Practice, Practice, Practice!

Shake and Step—Applications

If you've ever felt that the world was against you, but you must carry on and persevere and your determination to succeed cannot falter, this story is for you. It brings home the ideas of stick-to-it-tive-ness and persistence. It reminds us that even when a situation might *look* hopeless, there is still hope and the answer might lie in the midst of our own struggles. We came across a saying many years ago that read:

Whatever you vividly imagine, ardently desire, and enthusiastically act upon must eventually happen!

Your hard work and your determination to succeed will pay off for you. Quotes by two famous members of the British Empire express the same idea, even though the two people represent different eras:

"Never, never, never give in."—Sir Winston Churchill

"I will not even consider the possibility of defeat."—Queen Victoria

Three Key Applications

- Persistence
- Perseverance
- Looking for Alternatives

Shake and Step—The Story

A farmer is out working in his fields. He pauses briefly from his chores for a moment when he thinks he hears something. He listens but not hearing anything else is about to resume his work when there it is again—a faint squealing, almost a holler, as if it were a cry for help. He listens a bit more and, convinced that something is not right, halts his work and begins to move toward the sound. The farmer can tell that this cry is not human but coming from an animal somewhere on his property. He goes first to his barn only to discover nothing out of the ordinary. Then there it is again, louder this time. Definitely there is a problem; something is hurt or in distress. The farmer hurries from place to place checking his animals and all possible locations that come to mind. Then he suddenly recalls the old well—the old well he'd been meaning to fill in and cover for many years—the old well behind the original cabin on his farm—the old well that his wife had told him for more years than he cared to remember was an accident waiting to happen. He hurried over toward the well and as he approached, that sound came forth again. There was no mistaking it now, it was his old mule the General, and it was coming from the well.

Upon arriving at the well, which was long abandoned and no longer serving a purpose on the farm, he peered in. There was his old friend, his old mule, the General. Some how, some way, the General had fallen into the well. Fortunately, although cramped and a bit twisted, he had landed right side up and appeared to be okay. With some calming words, the farmer told the mule he would take care of him and have him out in no time. The poor animal moaned again. That mule had fallen down the well shaft over 20 feet and miraculously, with the exception of a few scrapes, was uninjured.

Uncertain as to what to do, the farmer decided to call his neighbor and ask for help. In less than 45 minutes, his neighbor was there surveying the situation. After another 30 minutes or so had passed, they still could not figure a way to get that old mule out of the abandoned well.

There was no telling exactly how long the mule had been down in the well, but his cries were getting more serious. After a great deal of deliberation and sadness, the farmers decided that all they could do was to fill the well in with dirt. This would put the old mule out of its misery and prevent further accidents from occurring.

The farmers reluctantly began their sad job of filling in the well, believing it to be the end of the faithful General. Now, something very interesting happened. Every time they pitched the dirt into the well, it would land on the back of the General and that mule didn't like it one bit. He would shake and step. That's right! He would shake off the dirt on his back and step on the dirt as it fell to the bottom of the well. This went on repeatedly for over two hours. The farmers worked hard pitching that dirt into the well and that mule just kept on shaking and stepping as each shovel full of dirt landed on him. When the dust cleared, the farmers stopped to survey what they had accomplished thus far. To their amazement upon looking down the well, there was the mule now only 5 or 6 feet from the surface. They had filled the well with over 15 feet of dirt, and that old mule just kept on shaking and stepping and was not about to be put to rest. The farmers now happily realized that the hole was going to be filled in and the General, as a result of his determination, was going to survive.

They resumed their work, and in less than another hour, they had filled in the abandoned well and the mule had, through its own perseverance, brought itself back to the top, a bit tired and with a few scrapes, but overall in remarkably good shape. The General slowly walked off to make his rounds as if this had been but a momentary distraction.

Other Insights:

Are you willing to stick it out?

- To persevere?
- To be committed to accomplishing your tasks?
- To shake it off and step up and move toward your goal?

Whatever you vividly imagine, ardently desire, and enthusiastically act upon must eventually happen!

The Dance—Applications

This story speaks of avoidance and risk taking. It speaks of how we are perceived and our perception of others, the words we use with others and the impact of these words upon them, and our ability to take on challenges and conflict and to grow from it and become stronger. This story reminds us of why some have learned to avoid taking risks and facing problems.

Three Key Applications

- Setting Goals
- Taking Risks
- Taking Action

The Dance—The Story

I can remember being a chaperone at a high school dance once and watching a boy come up to a girl to ask her to dance. Now, she is really pleased, but she's a freshman and hasn't been to too many of these functions. She looks out at the dance floor and there is only one other couple out on the floor. She says, "Well, I'd really like to dance, but could we just wait a little while until there are more people dancing?" Now, this boy, instead of listening to what she is really saying, takes her comment as a rejection. He replies, "Well that's okay. You're ugly anyway. So let's forget it." He walks back over to his friends and he's a "big man" and they have a laugh. But that girl is down here (hand gesture low to the floor), and it hurts so bad that it will take a long time to recover. Her confidence has been shattered.

Did you ever think about that person who is trying to put forth some extra effort at work because they care? Someone calls them a brown nose or misinterprets their actions and says something out of line. It hurts, and they back off. It has happened to us all. It doesn't take an individual long to realize that if they don't get involved, if they don't ask any questions, if they don't take any risks, then they won't feel any pain, they won't get embarrassed, and they won't get hurt.

That is so wrong because what happens is that we begin to build walls around ourselves—barriers to keep out the pain and the hurt. It doesn't take long until those walls get very thick and nothing can penetrate. The problem is that we don't let ourselves grow, learn, and experience life and change.

It is not too long until we realize that what we thought we had built as a fortress for protection in fact has become a prison.

Now is the time to act, set goals, take some risks, and strive for that excellence we are all capable of attaining.

Other Insights:

RISK

To laugh is to risk appearing the fool.
To weep is to risk appearing sentimental.
To reach out for another is to risk involvement.
To expose feelings is to risk exposing your true self.
To place your ideas, your dreams before the crowd
is to risk their loss.
To love is to risk not being loved in return.
To live is to risk dying.
To hope is to risk despair.
To try is to risk failure.
But, **risks must be taken** because the greatest hazard in life
is to risk nothing.
The person who risks nothing, does nothing, has nothing,
is nothing.
He may avoid suffering and sorrow,
But he simply cannot learn, feel, change, grow, love—live.
Chained by his certitudes, he is a slave.
He has forfeited freedom.
Only a person who risks is free.

—Anonymous

Risks must be taken!

What impact do you have on others with your choice of words?

Stop giving "killer statements."

Weigh negative criticism versus constructive feedback.

Don't build a fortress or a prison to reside in. Grow, learn, and experience life and change.

The Worst Day— Applications

Have you ever lost it and become so upset with someone that you've allowed your rationality to be overtaken by your anger? Someone once said that anger is like an acid; it can do more damage to the vessel in which it is stored than to the object on which it is poured. This story focuses us on what anger can do to us when we allow it to get a grip and a grasp upon us and how anger can destroy our ability to remain rational and think straight. If you are presenting a program dealing with anger-defusing techniques, conflict management, or uncomfortable situations, you will find this to be a powerful tool to capture the attention of your audience.

Three Key Applications

- Rationalizing
- Controlling Anger
- Responding

The Worst Day—The Story

A young woman approximately 28 years old had just had one of the worst days of her life. She and her husband had what many would categorize as the ideal marriage. They had been married for seven years, had a beautiful five-year-old son, and lived in a very comfortable home in a pleasant neighborhood. They had never had a serious argument, and they seemed to get along very well. It was a good marriage.

One evening it happened—a terrible argument. If you were to ask them today how it started, they couldn't even tell you exactly how it developed. A comment was made by one of them followed by a comeback remark, and it slowly escalated until, before they realized it, a serious argument was taking place. One thing quickly led to another and they were both shouting and quite angry with each other. Now, it was about 10:00 p.m. in the evening, and they had been preparing to go to sleep. They were both fuming as they got into their bed with their backs to each other—each still very upset as sleep slowly took hold. As soon as they awoke and made eye contact, the argument picked right up. They didn't skip a beat. The poor night's sleep simply added to the frustration and anger. Things continued to escalate.

The husband had to go to work that morning, so he quickly got ready and prepared for his day. During this time, comments were flying back and forth between the couple. Neither one was giving ground or attempting to sooth the situation. The husband stormed down the stairs and out the front door, slamming it as he walked toward his car. His wife followed him downstairs and, hearing the door slam, thought two can play that game, even though she was not leaving the house that day. She ran to the door quickly as her husband was just about to get into his car. She opened the door to the house and slammed it for him to hear as she went back inside. Take that, she thought! Her husband quickly backed down the driveway, narrowly missing the garbage cans at the end of the drive (which he usually brought up prior to leaving) and sped off.

This woman was beside herself. The anger had taken hold and she could barely contain herself. She decided that she had to talk to someone. She grabbed the telephone and phoned her best girlfriend and vented her feelings. Unfortunately, instead of just listening, her friend offered a lot of suggestions and advice. This resulted in the two of them becoming frustrated and quarreling, which simply added to the level of anger within the woman. She abruptly hung up, and the fire raging within her continued to burn. She had to do something to get her mind off the situation, so she decided to do some house cleaning. Selecting a rag, she began to dust. As she reached up to the top of a high ledge, she bumped a vase given to her by her grandmother. The vase toppled over and fell to the ground shattering. This was an irreplaceable family heirloom, and it just added to her anger.

All this had happened, and it was only 8:35 in the morning. She was upset to say the least. Her five-year-old son was totally unaware of the happenings of the night before and the escalation of events that morning. He was about to find himself in the wrong place, at the wrong time, with the wrong person—his own mother. He had very innocently come down the stairs carrying a few of his toys and his blanket. He went into the kitchen and opened the cabinet door containing many of the pots and pans and was playing while sitting on the kitchen floor. He bumped one of the pots and the chain reaction created quite a loud clamoring as many of the pots and pans tumbled onto the floor. It turned out to be the straw that broke the camel's back for the mother. She rushed into the kitchen, looked at her son, and said, "You go out into the backyard and get one of the sticks lying on the ground; you're going to get a beating." Well, of course, the young child was in tears, not grasping or understanding the situation. He obediently said, "Yes, Mommy," and headed outside. The mother was so out of control at this point that she was pacing back and forth. She didn't know what to do with herself as she waited for her son to return. She had lost it!

A few moments later, her son walked in. The tears were just rolling down his cheeks. He had his hands cupped in front of him as he turned to his mother and said, "Mommy, I couldn't find a stick. Will these do?" He had his hands filled with rocks.

That was all it took. Fortunately, the woman quickly regained her rationality as the anger just flowed away and reality set in. She rushed over to her son and embraced him—both of them were crying and the anger gone.

Other Insights:

Anger is not something we have to do. It is something we choose to do. Sometimes it can be a great challenge to remain calm and respond to a situation rather than allowing our emotions to take over and react. What are your anger hot buttons?

What symptoms in you are you aware of that occur when you are becoming angry? By identifying them, you have a better opportunity to place them in check and gain control over the situation and yourself by remaining rational.

What actions do you take when dealing with an irate or angry individual during an uncomfortable situation?

Until you are able to deal with anger, it is very difficult to focus on real issues. It's like standing before the Great Wall of China (representing anger). Until you are able to get over, under, around, or through that barrier you cannot get to the heart of the real situation and even begin to resolve the true problem.

Anger is a choice. You do not have to choose it!

Always Remember Those Who Serve—Applications

This story has many applications. It speaks of caring and concern for others while also demonstrating what can happen when we jump to conclusions in judging others too quickly.

Three Key Applications

- Caring
- Listening for Clarity of Understanding
- Responding

Always Remember Those Who Serve—The Story

In the days when an ice cream sundae cost much less, a ten-year-old boy entered a hotel coffee shop and sat at a table. A waitress put a glass of water in front of him. "How much is an ice cream sundae?" he asked. "Fifty cents," replied the waitress.

The little boy pulled his hand out of his pocket and studied the coins in it. "Well, how much is a plain dish of ice cream?" he inquired. By now more people were waiting for a table and the waitress was growing impatient. "Thirty-five cents," she brusquely replied. The little boy again counted his coins. "I'll have the plain ice cream," he said. The waitress brought the ice cream, put the bill on the table, and walked away. The boy finished the ice cream, paid the cashier, and left. When the waitress came back, she began to cry as she wiped down the table. There, placed neatly beside the empty dish, were two nickels and five pennies.

You see, he couldn't have the sundae because he had to have enough change left to leave her a tip.

—Anonymous

Other Insights:

When others are speaking to us, are we really listening to have clarity of understanding or are we just hearing? When we hear, we are taking in all the sounds around us, often misinterpreting and jumping to conclusions. When we listen, it is usually easier to properly respond to a situation because we are focusing our attention where it really needs to be.

It's easy to hear. All we have to do is basically exist and be there at the moment the sound is delivered. Listening takes caring and effort. It means putting your attention where it truly needs to be.

As a professional, you can be exhausted at the end of a day as a result of giving yourself permission to listen to your customer.

Always remember those who serve. Always remember those who care enough to give.

The Greatest Hurdler—Applications

This story is about goal setting—having a sense of direction. It has to do with taking aim and setting your sights on that final destination. If all you think about is what you don't want, that's exactly what you're going to get because you are creating it. Consider the following:

- Goal setting
- Overcoming obstacles
- Vision
- Mission
- Strategic objectives
- Core values
- Core competencies

Three Key Applications

- Setting Goals
- Having a Clear Vision and Mission
- Overcoming Obstacles

The Greatest Hurdler— The Story

A group of high school coaches are standing out by the front of the school observing various members of the high school track team during their workout. As Paul, a tenth-grade team member, approaches the coaches from his run around the building, he announces boldly, "I'm going to be the greatest hurdler in the history of the school." The coaches smile and continue their conversation, and Paul continues his run. On his second time around the school, as he nears the coaches, Paul announces, "I'm going to be the greatest hurdler in the history of the school," and he carries on.

Paul has caught the attention of one of the coaches, and that coach is determined to take Paul to task for his comment. As Paul approaches on his third lap around the school, the coach steps out to meet him and asks, "Paul, how are you going to be the greatest hurdler in the history of the school?" Paul, who was caught a bit off guard by the coach, stops and looks around as if searching for others who might be just a bit too near to overhear the answer to the question he has just been asked. So the coach looks around a bit, too. Paul asks, "Do you really want to know the secret?" "Yes, I do," says the coach. Paul takes a step back one more time as if checking the security of the area. The coach joins in and also looks around. Paul asks the coach to come closer. The coach moves closer to Paul as the young man is about to share his secret. "If you really want to know the secret of how to be the greatest hurdler in the history of the school, you go for the tape, you don't go for the hurdle; you go for the tape."

Paul repeats it one more time, "You go for the tape; you don't go for the hurdle." You go for the tape; you don't go for the hurdle! What philosophical words coming from that young tenth grader. We are all certainly going to have hurdles to overcome, but if we keep our sights set on the tape, we are going to get there.

Other Insights:

What hurdles do you have to overcome in your life?

What is the "tape" you're going for?

What are your mission, vision, and strategic objectives?

You need to go for the tape! You don't go for the hurdle—you go for the tape!

Message Received— Applications

This is a story guaranteed to bring forth some smiles while delivering an important message regarding behavior and performance. This story can be related to performance appraisals, delegation, responsibility, authority levels, and accountability that imply consequences. The message here is to be certain that one is praising the right performance for the right reasons while delivering the proper message.

Three Key Applications

- Knowing Your People
- Delegating Properly
- Praising Performance

Message Received— The Story

An infant who was not yet speaking, but was able to crawl and explore, would get in behind his father's valuable computer and stereo equipment. The father would admonish the infant each time by saying, "No, don't do that! If you do that, you will go to bed." This particular behavior occurred numerous times with the father repeating the statement each time, "No, don't do that! If you do that, you will go to bed."

As time went on, the child continued this particular behavior. Each time this performance was observed by the father, he would repeat his same mandate, "No, don't do that! If you do that, you will go to bed!" The behavior continued, and the child was learning to speak. His father observed him as he once again maneuvered behind the valuable equipment.

The father became so frustrated with this continued behavior that while directly looking into his son's eyes, he finally asked, "Why? Why do you keep going behind my valuable computer and audio equipment? Tell me why." The child looked lovingly up at his father and said, "Because I want to go to bed, Daddy!"

Other Insights:

The success of your organization depends on the performance of your people.

Are you giving your people the proper tools (responsibility, authority, and accountability) to achieve what you are asking of them?

Are you setting your people up for failure and building resentment and dissension?

To properly delegate, one must get to know their people so well that they are able to select the right person at the right time for the right task to achieve success.

The success of your organization depends on the performance of your people!

We Want Coffee— Applications

The customer must become the center of your organization. This story relates the critical importance of realizing that our customers want service, expect service, and demand service. If we are unable to extend that service to our customers, they will take their business elsewhere. This story is a wonderful tool to complement any program focusing on customer service and how significant the customer's perception of reality is.

Three Key Applications

- Customer Perception
- Excuses
- Customer Satisfaction

We Want Coffee—The Story

A few years ago, we were doing a presentation as part of a week-long workshop for a group of approximately fifty participants at a well-known hotel in Cleveland, Ohio. These workshop participants were real coffee drinkers; they went through three large containers of coffee and needed more. As an employee of the hotel was passing down the hall, one of the participants sitting in the back of the room near the door noticed him and said, "Excuse me. Could we please have some more coffee in here?" The hotel employee had the opportunity to respond by simply saying, "Yes, sir, I'll have that for you in a moment." That would have satisfied the plea being made and allowed for life to move along pleasantly. However, the hotel representative actually reacted by saying, "You know, I have four other meetings going on, three of my co-workers have called in sick today, one of our coffee machines is malfunctioning, and I'm not having my best day." Since our group had just been in the process of settling back into our session from a break, we all observed this moment of intense focus on so many items by this hotel employee except the one that critically needed his attention—the customer! We did not care about the other meetings. We did not care about those who didn't show up for work today. We didn't care that a machine was not working properly. We wanted coffee! We wanted service!

Other Insights:

Your customers want service! Excuses are those obstacles we ourselves create for not doing or avoiding those things we have an inherent responsibility to provide the customer with—excellent professional service in a caring, friendly, and consistent manner.

What is your customers' perception of the service you are delivering to them? Are you paying attention to that reality and using it to gauge your actions in treating your customers the way they want to be treated? How are you accomplishing this? How do you involve your customers in gauging your behavior, performance, or success?

Do you provide service or do you provide excuses?

The Hammer and the Fence— Applications

This is a wonderful story for dealing with anger and its impact on others. It also speaks of relationships and caring enough about someone else to take the required time necessary to produce lasting results. Someone going through a rough time in their life and having difficulty dealing with their own anger may find value in this story.

Three Key Applications

- Controlling Anger
- Damage Control
- Maintaining Focus

The Hammer and the Fence— The Story

A seventeen-year-old boy was noticeably having difficulty dealing with his anger, and it was getting progressively worse. His mother and father had observed a variety of behaviors they were not pleased with. Over the past month the young man, while upset over something, punched a hole in a wall in his room. On another occasion, he kicked the family dog out of frustration. His back talking and tone of voice with his parents and sisters was becoming progressively worse. The father decided it was time to take action.

On a Saturday morning as his son was getting up, the father said to the son, "When you're ready in a few minutes, I'd like you to meet me out in the backyard. We need to talk." His son said he would be right there, and in a short while, he joined his dad out in the yard. "Son, Mom and I couldn't help but notice that you've been having a difficult time dealing with your anger lately and it's not acceptable. By punching a hole in your wall, kicking Zeus (the dog), and back talking so much, you're hurting others and you're hurting yourself." "Dad, I know I haven't been dealing with things very well, but I don't know what to do about it. Sometimes I feel like I'm out of control." His father replied to this by saying, "Now, I know you're a good person and you've accomplished a lot of positive things at school and at home, but you need to tackle this behavior—this anger. I've got something I'd like you to give a try." His son said, "Okay Dad, I'll try. What's your idea?" The son noticed that his father was holding a hammer and a bag in his hand. Before he could question what those items were for, his dad said, "Every time you feel yourself getting angry, I want you to come out here by our fence (there was a large wooden fence around the entire backyard) and take a nail from this bag and pound it into the fence somewhere in this one section." His father indicated a portion of the fence to be used. "Every time you are angry, instead of taking that anger out on a wall or the dog or us, I want you to direct it to the fence as you pound that nail into it. I'd like you to do this for the next four weeks, and then we'll talk some more about your anger." "Okay, Dad, I'll do it. I know it has been a problem, and I'll really work at this," his son replied.

For the next month, the young man was very diligent. Every time anger was taking its toll, he would go out to the backyard and proceed to hammer a nail into the section of fence that had been so designated. At the end of the month, the father and son again found themselves in the backyard reviewing the results. The father started by saying, "Son, I'm really proud of you. You were really focused, and I can see the fence has many nails in it. Let's count them." Upon examination, it was determined that the son had driven a total of 58 nails into the fence. "What I would like you to do now," said the father, "is not just concentrate on redirecting your anger, but on stopping it. Every time you feel yourself getting angry and you are able to control it—because anger is not something we have to do but something we choose to do—I want you to come out here to the fence and pull one of those nails out. When you have pulled out the last nail, let me know and we will talk about this some more."

The son readily agreed and eleven weeks later (remember it had only taken four weeks to put 58 nails into the fence) he ran over to his dad and proclaimed, "Dad, I just pulled the last nail from the fence." His father once again told him how proud he was of him and how he had observed him working hard at controlling his anger. "Let's go back outside and take one more look at that fence," said the father. Once outside, they examined where the nails had been. The holes were obvious along with some other marks from the hammering. "Anger causes damage," the father said. Then he added, "Anger causes pain not only when you inflict it on your target but even when you make repairs. The damage that has been done leaves scars. Look at the nail holes—reminders of the anger that was there. Think how the fence would look if you had never driven in those nails in the first place. Think about the wall in your room, the dog, and our feelings when you raised your voice to us. By controlling anger before it gets the best of you, you get the best of it!" The son agreed, vowing never to let his anger control him again. He thanked his father and they went back into the house.

Other Insights:

- Think about the last time you were angry.
- What caused the anger?
- What were you thinking?
- How can you control your anger and remain in control?
- Can you share moments in your life when anger got the best of you? What were the results?
- Can you share a time where you controlled your anger? What were the results?

Anger causes damage, at times irreparable. The key is to stop it before the damage is done.

The Obstacle in Our Path—Applications

This is a story about caring, giving yourself permission to get involved, and doing something about a situation when it presents itself.

Three Key Applications

- Getting involved
- Caring
- Taking action

The Obstacle in Our Path— The Story

In ancient times, a king had a boulder placed on a roadway. Then he hid himself and watched to see if anyone would remove the huge rock. Some of the king's wealthiest merchants and courtiers came by and simply walked around it. Many loudly blamed the king for not keeping the road clear, but none did anything about getting the stone out of the way.

Then a peasant came along carrying a load of vegetables. Upon approaching the boulder, the peasant decided to try to move the stone to the side of the road. After much pushing and straining, he finally succeeded.

After the peasant picked up his load of vegetables, he noticed a purse lying in the road where the boulder had been. The purse contained many gold coins and a note from the king indicating that the gold was for the person who removed the boulder from the roadway. The peasant learned what many of us never understand.

What is that lesson?

Other Insights:

When you see a job that needs to be done, do it or at least ask what can I do to contribute? When applied to customer service, remember that delivering excellent customer service is everyone's job.

It's so easy to see a problem and avoid it, but to take the time to care, get involved, and do something about it reflects personal values and integrity.

Do whatever is right, necessary, proper, and just when it needs to be done.

Catching Monkeys— Applications

Change has been such a powerful topic, especially the past five years with mergers, acquisitions, upsizing, and downsizing. It has been quite a merry-go-round environment in corporate America, and not just for the companies, but for the individuals who make up each and every organization. With each change comes a transition—the personal, emotional, and psychological impact of change upon each one of us. This story can easily relate to change, transition, risk taking, the necessity of letting go, and the personal growth of new beginnings.

Three Key Applications

- Recognizing Change
- Letting Go
- Transitioning

Catching Monkeys— The Story

Many years ago, we had the opportunity to work with a Catholic nun, Sister Sebastia. Sister Sebastia was a delightful individual, and she had been a missionary in Africa for a number of years. She shared a story with us of a particular group of people and how they would capture monkeys. Sister Sebastia said that one individual would take a large gourd (slightly larger than a football) and he would cut an opening into this gourd about the size of a silver dollar. He would then proceed to carry this gourd to an area frequented by monkeys. He would hold up the gourd high for all the monkeys to see before placing it on the ground in an open area near a tree. He would then tether the gourd, tying it so that its movement was restricted and it could not be carried off.

The final act in this process was to walk over to a banana tree and select a banana and hold it up high for all to see as the man walked back to the gourd. He then placed the banana inside the gourd. Then he simply would back away to a safe, concealed distance. Eventually, one of these curious monkeys would come over to the gourd, examine it, give it a push, and check out the banana within. Now, there are bananas all around, all easily obtainable, but he wants that one. The monkey can easily put his hand into the small opening of the gourd and take his hand back out, as long as he did not grasp the banana. When the monkey grabbed the banana, he made a fist and he was trapped. Now his hand, which contained his prize, would not fit out of the hole, and there was no way that this monkey was going to release his prize. The monkey would make noise, jump around, and shake the gourd but not release his grip on the banana, thus remaining trapped. The person who had been watching from a distance now knew it was time to act. He simply walked over and, throwing a blanket over the monkey, caught the prey.

Sometimes, we find ourselves acting very similar to that monkey. We hold on to what we believe is our prize, our goal, our direction, and we won't let go for anything. No matter what changes might be going on around us, no matter what other ideas or advice are out there, we remain unchanging and—like that monkey—trapped. Unless we are willing to let go of that prize as we believe it to be, we cannot slip our bounds and move on and experience growth.

Other Insights:

The one thing in life that we know we can count on—the one constant factor—is change itself. How do you feel about change in your life and your business? Are you open to other ideas and suggestions? Are you willing to explore, dissect, and put to the test ideas that might be quite different from your own? Are you willing to become a change agent yourself?

Sometimes in order to grow to where we need to be, we must let go of where we are.

A Learning Experience— Applications

This wonderful short story speaks of enthusiasm, the tone of an individual's voice, the power of body language, and effectively communicating your message to the receiver.

Three Key Applications

- Expressing Enthusiasm
- Using Proper Body Language
- Delivering the Right Words

A Learning Experience—
The Story

Years ago, a high school teacher was having a discussion with a group of seniors concerning effective communication and getting your message across. He asked one of the senior boys, "When you are at home sitting around the dinner table, what are some typical questions your father might ask you about your day?" The young man thought about this for a moment and then said, "My dad might say, 'How was school today?'" "And, how would you typically respond to that question?" asked the teacher. "Well," said the senior, "I would usually just say, 'Okay,' and go on eating." "What else might your father ask?" the teacher further inquired. The student pondered this and replied, "My dad often asks me, 'What did you do at school today?' And, I simply say, 'Oh, nothing.'" The teacher smiled, as did the other students in the group. The teacher then said, "Tonight, when you go home and you're sitting with your family having dinner and your father asks, 'How was school today?' I want you to try something new. I want you to suddenly stand and face your father, and with your shoulders back and while looking directly at your father, say, 'Dad, today was the single most significant learning experience of my entire life!' I want you to say it sincerely and enthusiastically, and I want you to tell us how your father responded and your observations tomorrow." "Okay, I'll do it!" said the student as the bell rang indicating the end of class.

The next day, the high school senior could hardly wait for that particular class to take place. The teacher picked up his discussion on effective communication and asked if anyone had something to share from yesterday's discussion. The young man could hardly contain himself as he excitedly shared with the class what had occurred around his family's dinner table the past evening. "We're sitting there having dinner. It's fairly quiet because everyone is really enjoying my mom's fried chicken, when my dad said to me, 'So how was your day at school today?' I suddenly pushed my chair back, stood up tall with my shoulders back, and looked right at my dad. 'Dad,' I said, 'today was the single most significant learning experience of my entire life!'" Everyone in the class was laughing but curious. "What did your father say, and what did you observe?" asked the teacher. The senior replied, "Well, it was pretty amazing. My dad fell right out of his chair!"

Other Insights:

The words we use and how we deliver them can have a significant impact on the way they are received.

Does anyone have a story to share about miscommunication and the resulting confusion or misunderstanding that took place?

How can we ensure that a message is received and understood?

Why is repeating back and summarizing so important?

What responsibilities does the sender of a message have?

What about the receiver?

Make it the single most significant learning experience of your entire life!

The Pledge—Applications

You may choose the most beautiful words, but it is the way you *use* those words—your tone of voice, delivery, and articulation—that can make all the difference in the world. This story has to do with the power of words, the way in which a message is received and interpreted. Effective communication is magic and the proper delivery of ideas from one individual to another requires thought, patience, and concern for the receiver.

Three Key Applications

- Receiving Messages
- Interpreting Messages
- Delivering the Right Words

The Pledge—The Story

A man was driving home from work one evening. It had been a good day, but a tiring one. He turned on the radio, and the DJ he usually listened to at this hour was just getting into another of his entertaining contests. "I need three listeners to call in; we're going to try something a little different tonight."

Three individuals responded by calling in quickly, eager to participate. The man driving home was curious about what was to follow. The DJ explained, "I'm going to read something to you, which you will all quickly recognize. It is the Pledge of Allegiance. I'm going to read it very sincerely and patriotically, reflecting caring and concern. After I have finished, I'm going to ask Caller Number One to say those exact same words that I just read, except this time I want you to say the Pledge as if you were very angry. Caller Number Two, I want you to say the Pledge as if you were hysterical, and Caller Number Three, I want you to say the Pledge as if you were very sad."

All the callers acknowledged their understanding of the task, and the DJ proceeded to state very sincerely and with great care the words we are all so familiar with. *"I Pledge Allegiance to the Flag of the United States of America..."* Even though he had heard the words of the Pledge hundreds, if not thousands, of times, the words evoked pride, patriotism, and love of country each time the driver heard them and tonight driving home was no exception.

"Caller Number One, you're up!" said the DJ, who also focused the driver's attention back to the radio once more. In a loud, emotionally charged, stern voice, Caller Number One said the same words of the Pledge, which had just been spoken so eloquently. What a difference! The anger blotted out the words, and the focus turned to the messenger, not the message. The same was true for Caller Number Two's hysterical rendition; the caller screeched and squealed the words of the Pledge as if she were bouncing off walls and totally out of control. Caller Number Three outdid all that preceded him. He recited the Pledge in tears as if a great weight were on his shoulders. The sadness was portrayed so well that the driver couldn't help but feel moved by this individual and sad for him.

Wow, the driver thought as he listened. It really did make a difference in the way the message was received. You can have the most beautiful words in the world, but the way you deliver those words can make all the difference.

The program he had been tuned in to had been focusing on effective communication and listening. The contest, if you could actually call it that—perhaps more a demonstration—made a great deal of sense now, and it really struck home. You see, the man driving was a corporate trainer, and his main focus this past month had been developing a program on effective communication.

Other Insights:

Do you choose your words wisely when speaking to others and give proper time and thought as to how those words will be delivered? Periodically, you may wish to record a conversation you're having with a co-worker and then do a self-evaluation of your own delivery of the content. Were you sincere? Did the receiver interpret your message in the way you had intended? Again, your tone, your articulation, the emotions you display, and other nonverbal communication impact tremendously the way your words are received. The spoken word, once spoken, is very difficult if not impossible to take back. It certainly is worth your time and consideration as you communicate effectively with others.

You may have the most beautiful words in the world, but the way you deliver those words can make all the difference.

Getting Enough Air?— Applications

This story relates to effective communication—saying what you mean and meaning what you say. It emphasizes thinking about what you have to say, and ensuring that the message you are sending has been received and interpreted in the manner in which you intended it to be received.

Three Key Applications

- Effectively Communicating
- Sending the Proper Message
- Interpreting What You Hear

Getting Enough Air?— The Story

It was finally Saturday. Everyone had had such a terribly difficult, challenging, and exhausting work week. It was time to have some fun, and a group of friends, five married couples, had been planning a weekend trip to the mountains—with hiking, camping, and sharing their great friendship—for the past month.

John and Heather had volunteered their home as the base camp for all the five married couples to meet. Bill and Emily, Don and Rachael, Chad and Vicky, and Jan and Tom would all be arriving shortly, and it was only 7:00 a.m. John was loading the camping equipment into their jeep and finishing final preparation when the others began arriving. They were all smiles, all excited, and ready for a great weekend.

All the married couples were now present when Heather came walking out of the house holding the human interest social section of the morning newspaper. "Have you seen the headline in the newspaper this morning?" exclaimed Heather. All replied in the negative. They had been so enthused about the weekend and getting ready that no one had taken the time to even glance at the newspaper. "Well, look at this!" said Heather. The newspaper headline in large bold letters proclaimed **Seven out of every 10 married couples may be having an affair.** Now, the guys smiled, waved their hands in the air and got back to work preparing to leave. The ladies, however, proceeded into the house and continued to discuss the matter in more detail.

It's now 9:00 p.m. Sunday evening, and the five married couples have all had an incredible time together. The weather had been perfect. They had the best time, and now each couple was returning home. As they are driving the last five miles to their house, Heather turns to John and says, "That was quite a story wasn't it?" Now John has no idea what Heather is speaking of and responds with "What story?" Heather qualifies her question by explaining, "You know. That story I showed everyone on Saturday morning. The one that said seven out of every ten married couples may be having an affair." "I didn't give that any thought at all with all that we had going on," said John. "Well, I have. And quite a bit!" said Heather. John, being caught off guard and now with a puzzled look on his face replied, "You have. Why?" Heather explained, "Well, you know there were ten of us together this weekend, five married couples. And if those statistics are correct that seven out of every ten married couples may be having an affair, then some of our very best friends may…" John cut off Heather before she could finish her statement. "Heather, come on. You can't believe that story." Before Heather could even comment, John decided he would strategically bring this discussion to a rapid conclusion. He said, "You know Heather, if you really believe that story has any truth to it, when we get home, why don't we take out a pen and paper and write down the names of all our married friends and between us decide just who may be having an affair." John believes that Heather will see the absurdity of this and say don't be ridiculous, and that will be the end of this nonsense. To John's amazement, Heather's reply is not what he expected at all. "That's a great idea; let's do it," says Heather. John realizes he has created a monster and he had now painted himself into a corner. As they pulled into their garage and parked the car, Heather grabbed a few items, and as she walked toward the door to their house states, "You unpack and I'll get things ready inside." Little does John realize that Heather is still thinking about that newspaper headline, ***Seven out of every 10 married couples may be having an affair.*** She's thinking about the conversations that went on with the other wives in the kitchen, on the trail, and around the campfire. She's thinking about that list that John had suggested they build and discuss together.

As John comes into the house, Heather shouts to him from the living room, "Honey, I've got the pad and paper and as soon as you're ready, come on over here." John knows he isn't going to get out of this and thinks to himself let's get this over and get to bed. John joins Heather in their living room, and within 15 minutes, they have put together a list with 17 married couples they know, all friends and all fitting the criteria of the news story. They go back to the top of the list and review each name discussing their thoughts on whether this individual may be having an affair. It goes something like this: "Okay, how about Bill or Emily?" "Absolutely not!" They both agree emphatically and move on. "What about Chad or Vicky?" "Well not Chad, but what about Vicky?" They place a question mark next to Vicky's name and smile with a raise of the eyebrows and move on. They proceed through the entire list until John believes they are each satisfied and can now put it aside and get to bed.

John and Heather proceed upstairs to get ready for bed. John is again thinking of the great times they had with their friends this weekend and how fortunate they are to know such good people. Heather's thoughts are elsewhere. She's still thinking about that headline, **Seven out of every 10 married couples may be having an affair.** She is still reviewing all the discussions with her girlfriends, and now she's pondering the list she and John have just finished and discussed, realizing that there were two names they had not put on the list: her's and John's. She didn't really want to consider it; she had a wonderful marriage, but as a result of all that had taken place, she wondered if John was happy, if….

Now, one side note needs to be shared here. John and Heather do not have air conditioning. Their home is at a higher elevation (about 6,000 feet) in one of the more mountainous states, and air conditioning had not been necessary. It had, however, been a warmer summer than usual.

John prefers to sleep with the windows wide open. He loves fresh air. However, tonight it is slightly cooler than the past week had been, and he knows Heather prefers the windows to be closed with just a slight opening. Thinking of Heather and being a kind, loving husband, he lowers the windows leaving a small opening for air.

John and Heather get into bed. Each is pretty tired now, and they look forward to a good night's rest. They lie down, each with their own thoughts—John still focused on the absolutely incredible time they had with their dear friends and Heather still caught up with the thoughts she simply cannot let go of. She's thinking about that newspaper article, **Seven out of every 10 married couples may be having an affair.** She is going over her discussions with her friends and thinking about that list she and John had compiled. She's also thinking about her own marriage.

She suddenly turns to John and asks, "John, are you having an affair?" but what John, starting to drift off, hears is "John are you getting enough air?" John responds by saying, "Of course I am honey, aren't you?" Heather screams and runs from the room. John, totally in a state of confusion now looks around the room and shouts, "Honey, I'll lower them (the windows) even more if you like!"

It took Heather and John the next hour to calm down and get things settled: to figure out what Heather had actually asked and what John thought he had heard, then to understand what Heather thought John was responding to and so on. What a weekend and what a night!

Other Insights:

We need to be certain that what we think we are hearing is actually what has been stated. Only then can we properly respond to the statement just delivered.

Have you ever found yourself in a situation where, as a result of not hearing or listening properly to what was being said, a misinterpretation took place resulting in a misunderstanding? What is your story?

Why is listening so critical and how can we become better listeners?

What is the difference between hearing and listening?

One of the greatest courtesies we can extend to another person is to listen to them!

Giving When It Counts—Applications

Caring, love for your fellow man, having a passion for what you do, and being willing to make sacrifices for the success of others are some of the applications for this story, which will touch your heart.

Three Key Applications

- Having a Passion
- Making Sacrifices
- Delivering Excellence

Giving When It Counts— The Story

Many years ago, when I worked as a volunteer at a hospital, I got to know a little girl named Liz who was suffering from a rare and serious disease. Her only chance of recovery appeared to be a blood transfusion from her five-year-old brother, who had miraculously survived the same disease and had developed the antibodies needed to combat the illness. The doctor explained the situation to her little brother, and asked the little boy if he would be willing to give his blood to his sister. I saw him hesitate for only a moment before taking a deep breath and saying, "Yes, I'll do it if it will save her."

As the transfusion progressed, he lay in bed next to his sister and smiled, as we all did seeing the color returning to her cheeks. Then his face grew pale and his smile faded. He looked up at the doctor and asked with a trembling voice, "Will I start to die right away?" Being young, the little boy had misunderstood the doctor. He thought he was going to have to give his sister all of his blood in order to save her.

You see, after all, understanding and attitude are everything.

Other Insights:

What sacrifices are we willing to make for those things we truly believe in?

What would we be willing to give our very lives for?

Do you truly have a passion for your customers and your pursuit of delivering excellence?

"I don't necessarily have to like my associates, but as a man, I must love them. Love is loyalty, love is teamwork, and love respects the dignity of the individual. Heart power is the strength of your corporation."

—Vince Lombardi

Talk'n About Me, Weren't You?—Applications

This lighthearted story reflects the ideas of perception, humor, and creativity and can add a refreshing bit of air to a more tense moment when some relief is needed. We have observed this story being used in discussions referring to paradigms, creative thinking, human interaction, and practical risk taking.

Three Key Applications

- Creative Thinking
- Interacting
- Risk Taking

Talk'n About Me, Weren't You?—The Story

The high school basketball team had made it to the state tournament, and even though they had not captured the championship, they placed well. It had been the most successful year in sports their school had ever attained. What a wonderful time of school spirit, camaraderie, and moments they would never forget.

One side activity they had been able to experience while at the state capital was a trip to the Natural History Museum. While the group was on the elevator going from the seventh floor to the fourth floor, one of the team members, a young tenth grader standing near the door, turned and faced the rest of the group as the elevator doors opened on the sixth floor. "It's been wonderful meeting with all of you here today, and I thank you all for coming to this gathering," exclaimed the youth, who slowly backed out as the doors closed. Most of the others had puzzled looks on their faces and one said, "What was that all about?" The elevator continued down as other comments were heard regarding the odd behavior.

Now, unbeknownst to those on the elevator, the young man who had just departed had a plan of action. As the group had boarded the elevator, not only had he pushed the fourth floor button on the side panel while saying out loud, "All aboard for the fourth floor," but he had also pushed the fifth and sixth floor buttons as well.

The elevator stopping on the sixth floor put his plan into motion as he faced the group, slowly stepping backward and making his statement. As the doors closed, he quickly made his way down the stairs to the fourth floor, knowing that having also pushed the fifth floor button would give him the necessary time to complete his mission. The elevator stopped and the doors opened on the fifth floor with no one getting on or off. In a moment, the doors closed and the elevator moved to the fourth floor. As the doors opened, there stood the young tenth grader, again facing his startled companions. "Bet you were talk'n about me, weren't you?" he exclaimed to the laughter of the group.

Other Insights:

Sometimes stepping out of the box and doing things in a different manner can create a whole new perspective for us.

Have you ever taken a totally different route home than the way you usually travel and notice all the surroundings? Then, when you return to your usual route, do you notice the changes, buildings, trees, and other items you never had observed before?

How do you think outside the box?

Creativity may be the only discernable difference you have or your company has between you and the competition.

Out of our creative minds and potential risk taking develops our future. Remember the old expression, "If you always do what you've always done, then you'll always get what you've always got!"

Creativity may be the only discernable difference between you and the competition.

Our New Car—Applications

This story focuses on perception—not only on how we see or view the world around us but how others perceive it. It relates to using our judgment and not being too quick to pass judgment on others until we have gathered all the facts and truly understand the circumstances of a situation.

Three Key Applications

- Your Perception
- Customer's Perception
- Reality

Our New Car—The Story

A hardworking, very proud man had a great deal of misfortune. He had a heart attack, and as a result of poor medical coverage along with some investments that just didn't work out well, his family practically lost everything. As a result of all these unfortunate circumstances, this man was forced to go on welfare. Again, he was a very proud, caring gentleman whose children didn't realize until years later how poor they really had become or how ill their father was.

One day, the father and his son stopped off at a grocery store to purchase a few items. They only bought those items they absolutely needed. Nothing frivolous was placed in the cart. The father was embarrassed because he was purchasing the items with food stamps and was very careful to purchase what he believed to be appropriate items. While waiting in the checkout line, a man who was a few people behind them noticed the food stamps that the boy's father was holding. He had taken them out to be prepared so that they could move through the checkout as quickly as possible. The man began to voice his opinion. He was rather belligerent and loudly began complaining about the system and the economy and the government and all the people who abused his tax dollars, which he worked so hard for.

This man did not let up. He kept on complaining, becoming rather abusive, and his language and comments reflected his feelings. He was obviously directing his tirade at the father and son in front of him. The father remained quiet while his young son was thinking, "Dad, why don't you pop this guy?" His father was a pretty big man and a very imposing figure. But the father remained silent, taking care of business, and he and his son proceeded out of the store.

Just prior to all the misfortune that had befallen the father, he had purchased a brand new car with his hard-earned money. This had occurred five months ago right before the heart attack. He had decided to keep the car, which was paid for, and was planning for it to be the family car for many years to come. As they approached their car and began placing the groceries in the trunk, they heard the voice of the obnoxious man from the store once again. He had exited the store soon after them and had observed them by their new car—buying groceries with food stamps and then walking out to a beautiful new car.

The guy who had been so rude in the store went ballistic. He continued on with his insults saying, "Some people don't know the meaning of work. All they do is take advantage of others. What the ?X!O?X!O (expletives!) right do you have to be driving a car like that. You lazy so and so. How do you have the nerve to even shop in the same store as people like me?" He went on and on and on. The son thought, "Okay, this is going to be good. Go get him Dad!" To his surprise his father remained silent, finished putting the items into the car, motioned for his son to get in, and drove off. The next ten minutes were spent in total silence. As they came up to a red light and stopped, the father turned to his son and said, "Don't you ever judge someone until you know the whole story."

Other Insights:

Perception plays such a powerful role in the way we view things. When dealing with our customers in our business, remember that it is the customer's perception of reality that really counts. If they perceive our service and behavior to be excellent and focused on their needs, they will tend to continue the relationship. If, on the other hand, their perception is one of poor or inadequate service—service that does not focus on them and their needs—they will tend to take their business elsewhere.

How do you determine your customer's perception of reality?

What environment does your customer perceive when they enter your place of business or speak to you over the phone?

Don't ever judge another until you know the entire story.

Please, Sorry, Love, and Thanks—Applications

This story is an excellent closing for a meeting, workshop, retreat, or any learning experience when the participants have worked and grown together. It is meant to remind individuals that when a training session ends, the learning and reinforcement of the knowledge and skills presented must continue on. Only with proper practice will the items covered in a classroom become part of a person's normal everyday behavior.

Three Key Applications

- Giving Yourself Permission
- Sharing
- Accepting

Please, Sorry, Love, and Thanks—The Story

We have a dear friend who is a minister, and he tells us that he has observed four things that people often say when they kneel down to pray: *please, sorry, love,* and *thanks*.

I have to say please. Please give yourself permission to make a difference. Please give yourself permission to take the knowledge and skills we have discussed and developed in this book and make them become part of your normal everyday behavior. Only you can give yourself permission to do this. Please share what you have learned with others and apply what you have learned.

I have to say sorry. I'm sorry that the television news cameras of the world will most likely not cover your story. Remember that others are aware of the good things you are doing (your company, co-workers, family, etc.), but even more important, you are aware of what you have accomplished and what you are all about.

I have to say love. Love the good things you face each day and even the negatives. We have to accept and deal with everything that life presents us each day: the good, the bad, and the ugly—the total package. Have a passion for what you do for the good of your co-workers and your customers, both internal and external.

And I have to say thanks. Thanks for your participation in, involvement in, and commitment to success, achievement, and growth. Thanks for all that you have done in the past, for what you're doing right now, and for all you're going to do.

Other Insights:

When a meeting or training session concludes, the "ball is in your court" so to speak for each individual participant. The choice is theirs to simply end it there and return to exactly what they were doing or to use the material and ideas covered and take it to an even higher level by putting it to the test. The decision is really up to each individual to make it happen. The choice is theirs to bring the knowledge and skills covered to life through practice and application or allow them to slowly be forgotten.

Training is not just training's responsibility. Training is everyone's responsibility.

The Little Bitty Frying Pan—Applications

This short story relates to goal setting and goal achievement. The need to give the appropriate thought and consideration to the goals we are setting must be defined in order to ensure the "right fit." The boundaries you establish must coincide with and support your goals.

Three Key Applications

- Setting Appropriate Goals
- Choosing Challenges
- The "Right Fit"

The Little Bitty Frying Pan—The Story

An individual is walking down by the fishing piers and he sees a fisherman casting out his line. As he draws nearer, he observes that as the fisherman is catching fish, he is throwing away the big fish (letting them go back into the ocean) and keeping the small ones. This seems rather odd to the observer. He watches this activity go on for quite a while. He then walks up to the fisherman and asks him, "I've been watching you and you're really catching a lot of fish there. I couldn't help but notice that you let the big fish go, and you only keep the small fish. Why is that?" The fisherman looked at the person and said, "All I've got at home is a little bitty frying pan."

Other Insights:

Big goals make us reach in and use the resources we have within. Be certain to set goals that properly challenge and encourage growth.

Set goals that will challenge you and encourage growth.

The Mariner—Applications

This story has to do with focus of attention. It asks us to think about our commitments to what we have chosen to do with our lives. Do we have a passion for our work, the tasks before us, and even those we work with?

Three Key Applications

- Focusing
- Being Committed
- Achieving Potential

The Mariner—The Story

There once was an old sailor, a mariner. He was regaling a group of people who had gathered around him down by the shipping docks. "I have been a mariner all my life," he proclaimed. "For over 40 years I have sailed the seas and learned all there is to know about the ocean."

A young man questioned the mariner by asking, "You know the ocean do you? What really lies beneath it? What is contained in the ocean's depths?" "I don't really know the answer to that," said the mariner.

"So you have just skimmed the surface all these years," the young man replied as he walked off.

Other Insights:

Often as a professional, we just skim the surface of what lies before us. Just going through the routine motions of our duties is not sufficient to truly achieve our potential. We need to delve deeper and push ourselves to more fully explore the true limits of our capabilities.

What does it truly mean to be a professional?

To fully achieve our potential, we must delve deep below the surface of our professionalism.

Building Bridges— Applications

This story has many applications: dealing effectively with anger, relationship building, team building, being a builder rather than a destroyer of those items necessary for interpersonal relationships. The story also has some spiritual applications.

Three Key Applications

- Dealing with Anger
- Building Relationships
- Having a Magnificent Obsession

Building Bridges— The Story

Two brothers who were farmers were given large amounts of land from their father. The two properties were adjacent to each other with a beautiful river running between separating the brothers' land. Each brother built a magnificent home facing the other's home across the river. The two brothers got along very well and helped each other with the running and operation of their farms. One day the brothers had a disagreement and it escalated into an argument. They were each so upset that they left vowing never to speak to the other again. One brother even remarked that he didn't even want to ever see his brother or for that matter his house or property again.

These feelings did not dissipate as time went on. A year passed with the brothers not speaking or associating with each other. Each evening they would sit out on their front porches and look across the river at the other's farm. The one brother who could not even bear to see the other would often get up and go inside ranting and raving over the fact that he even had to look out across the river to see his brother and his home.

That evening while at home, still fuming over his feelings of anger toward his brother, there came a knock at the door. Now in this area, there were not many visitors, and the man thought perhaps, it's my brother! He goes to the door opening it with a quick pull ready to do battle. To his surprise it is not his brother, but a man in his early thirties. "Good evening, Sir. I am a skilled carpenter by trade, as was my father. I am looking for work. Do you happen to be in need of someone with my skills?" Well, this was exactly what the brother had been looking for. "You have come at a very opportune time. I do have work for you," he said. He offered the carpenter a place to sleep for the evening and some food and, because of the late hour, said they would get started in the morning.

Early the next morning, the brother and the carpenter met to discuss the project. "I'm going to be gone for the next three weeks. I have urgent business to attend to," said the brother. "I want you to build a high fence in front of my house, high enough and long enough so that I cannot see my brother's house across the river. Can you do that?" "It will be as you wish," said the carpenter.

Shortly afterward, the brother left on his journey greatly anticipating the finished project upon his return. The three weeks passed slowly for the brother as he met with various people over farming matters. He could not stop thinking about the fence being built by the carpenter. No longer would he have to even look at his brother or his possessions. His anger was still with him.

At the conclusion of his work in town, the brother hurried home, anticipating seeing the large barrier. As he approached his land, he strained his eyes scanning the area to the front of his home. Nothing! How could this be? Where was the carpenter? He would certainly pay for his deception. However, there was something new near his home spanning the river. He had not noticed it at first because he had been so intent on seeing the fence. Reaching across the river was a beautifully carved wooden bridge. What on earth was the meaning of this? He ran to the bridge rather amazed at how beautiful it was. It was difficult to be upset with such craftsmanship. Suddenly there at the other end of the bridge stood his brother. All the anger and ill feelings seemed to dissolve as the two men approached each other, now running, and finally embracing. His brother said to him, "What a beautiful bridge you have built, truly a symbol of our love for each other and that nothing can keep us apart. Even our lands are now connected. Let us forgive our past disagreements and let this bridge symbolize our unity." The brother was overjoyed by these words and agreed while saying, "We must celebrate this moment and we must include the builder of this awesome structure that has brought us together."

He ran back to his home searching for the carpenter. He looked everywhere and was about to give up hope when he noticed off in the distance someone walking away from the farm. It was the carpenter. He ran shouting, and only with continued shouts and exhibiting great effort was he able to finally capture the carpenter's attention. As he walked over to him he said, "Carpenter, what you have done here is truly a miracle, for my brother and I have been angry with each other for too long and now all is forgiven and forgotten. How can I ever repay you for what you have done? Please come with me and join us as we celebrate this evening. You will be our honored guest." The carpenter smiled and replied, "Your being together once again with your brother is payment enough, and I am honored at your invitation to celebrate your reunion. Unfortunately, I cannot stay. There is much work to be done. I have many bridges to build!" And, with those words, he departed.

Other Insights:

What bridges need to exist between those within your organization?

How do you bridge the gap between these groups?

Questions to ponder:

- Are we accomplishing what we set out to do?
- Did we do what we said we were going to do?
- Did we keep our sites on our goal(s)?
- Do we have a magnificent obsession?
- Did we build the right kind of bridge?

    Building bridges between:

    Community (Image) ------------ Company
    Department ---------------------- Department
    Division -------------------------- Division
    Associate ------------------------ Associate
    Company ------------------------ Customer

Are you a bridge builder or a bridge destroyer?

What bridges need to be built within your organization, team, or family?

Planes, Ships, and People—Applications

This story reflects on goal setting and, most importantly, goal achievement. Yes, there are some dangers in setting goals because we must confront our fears. Each of us must find the strength and courage to take practical risks and give ourselves permission to take action and do what must be done to achieve our goals, realizing our true potential. The possible dangers that lurk in the shadows are significantly greater when we do not set any goals at all or fail to take action.

Three Key Applications

- Goal Setting
- Goal Achievement
- Practical Risks

Planes, Ships, and People— The Story

Did you know that an airplane will wear out much faster by simply having it sit on the ground rather than fly in the air? Planes are made to fly! They reach their full potential when used for that purpose for which they were built.

A ship in a harbor will rust and wear out much faster than when it is out in the open sea. Ships are made to sail! Only then do they achieve the full limit of their potential for which they were built.

We are not perfect beings; we are human beings. However, we each possess unique skills and talents that are intended to be used. Only then can we exercise and nurture these items to continually grow and achieve. It is only through the setting and the achievement of goals that the cause (purpose) that each of us has identified may be realized. To not set goals, to not challenge ourselves, to not have a cause that moves us forward can be devastating to our very existence. Each one of us desperately needs to actively use all that has been bestowed upon us. We were made to use what we've got!

Other Insights:

Take a moment right now and list the talents, skills, and gifts you possess— items that you bring to your workplace, home, family, and friends. With those items you just listed in mind, focus on three goals you want or need to accomplish in each of those categories. Next, under each goal listed, come up with three specific activities that when taken and accomplished by you will move you toward that particular goal. They will assist in establishing your personal cause or vision.

What is your personal cause or vision? Where do you intend to be in the next five years? How will you achieve that? What are you intending to do over the next two years that will complement and support your master cause covering the five-year period. Does your two-year plan move you toward your five-year cause? If so, you're heading in the right direction. If not, please revisit these items. Why are you seeking to accomplish these items if they are not part of your master plan—your cause? What about what you're doing this year? Do your yearly goals align with your two-year and five-year plans? Is it a journey that is mapped out and meaningful or one filled with the attitude of whatever happens, happens? You are in control of you if you so choose to be—your direction, your goals, your cause, and your ultimate success!

Don't just be a goal setter. Be a goal achiever.

Dynamite—Applications

This story deals with self-reflection, soul searching, and taking a good hard look at that one person we often have the most difficult time focusing on: our self. A self-analysis at times can be a reality shock. What course or direction have you set for yourself in life and how will it be perceived by others as well as yourself?

Three Key Applications

- Self-reflection
- Setting a Direction
- Perception by Others

Dynamite—The Story

This story begins with the question, who invented dynamite? The answer is Alfred Nobel. He did this with the very best of intentions in mind. He envisioned dynamite helping to remove obstacles for building highways, constructing tunnels through mountains, and demolishing old, unsafe buildings to make way for new structures. There were a multitude of positive reasons for which Alfred felt that dynamite would be a useful, beneficial gift to mankind.

Alfred Nobel drastically changed the perception he had of himself and of his invention. Alfred's brother passed away, and a local newspaper in his town made the mistake of not printing his brother's obituary but instead ran the obituary of Alfred himself. Alfred awoke that morning to read his own obituary in the paper and what he read devastated him. It read: "Died, Alfred Nobel—the inventor of dynamite, that deadly and destructive force used in warfare and the killing of people. It is one of the most deadly and destructive forces known to mankind."

Alfred was so dismayed by these words and the images they brought to mind that he experienced a life-changing moment. He was to spend the rest of his life dedicated to altering the negative image he had received from that newspaper article. Through the promotion of outstanding achievements in the fields of physics, chemistry, physiology, medicine, literature, and economics, and for the promotion of world peace, Alfred certainly did change that original image we may have all been left with. Today when we think of the name and of the man Alfred Nobel, we think of the Nobel Peace Prize that he founded for the accomplishments in the areas just mentioned.

Other Insights:

If you were able to read your own obituary today, would you be pleased with what it would say? If not, what are you doing to change that final accumulation of printed words on the life you have led? If you are pleased with the words of that obituary, then we commend you. Go in peace!

One additional insight on the topic of the Nobel Peace Prize: Mother Theresa, a recipient of this honored prize, did not participate in the gala affairs celebrating the award. She said that she greatly appreciated the award, but had too much work still to be accomplished to take the precious time needed to attend the functions. She had a beautiful statement to conclude her thoughts on this matter, "God has written a love letter, and I am but a pen in his hand."

What course or direction have you set for yourself in life and how will it be perceived by others?

Rear View Mirror— Applications

We all need to make certain that we have not left anything out or any item still to be uncovered as we take on a new challenge or task. We must thoroughly analyze and dissect a situation or problem to achieve a complete understanding of that problem so as to initiate the proper solution. We must give the proper thought to a project or goal before moving ahead and taking action. Question, think, evaluate, and reflect on a situation so that we can properly respond rather than react.

Three Key Applications

- Analyzing and Dissecting
- Strategizing
- Proceeding with Confidence

Rear View Mirror—
The Story

A young man had just turned sixteen, and his father was teaching him how to drive. The boy was doing very well, but he had one area of disagreement with his father that was to last a number of years.

The father insisted that you not only have to adjust your rear view and side mirrors to accommodate for blind spots, but that you also need to look over your shoulder to really cover all the hidden areas. The son insisted that by positioning and adjusting the mirrors properly, all blind spots would be covered, thus eliminating the need to look over the shoulder.

This disagreement lasted a number of years until one day the son came across an article containing information from a car manufacturer and various driving experts that supported his belief. It contended that all blind spots could indeed be eliminated with the proper use of the rear view and side mirrors. The son cut out the article and sent it to his father.

The father upon receiving the material from his son was quick to counter with his own information supporting his side of the argument and continued to insist that the mirrors did not cover all the required areas.

Stand before a full-length mirror and consider your own blind spots whenever you are accepting a new challenge, task, position, or whatever journey you are about to embark upon. Have you got it all covered? What are you missing? What is not being seen properly and still requires clarity of understanding? What can be seen but perhaps has not been properly appreciated—especially what can be seen in that rear view mirror—shows us where we have been and the long road already traveled to allow ourselves to get to where we are today! Enjoy the journey!

Other Insights:

Where have you been?

Where are you going?

How are you going to get there?

Do you have a plan of action—a strategy for success?

Have you carefully thought through each step in your journey and does it make sense?

If so, proceed with confidence.

**Where have you been?
Where are you going?
How are you going
to get there?**

Everything is Just Fine!—Applications

Effective listening takes hard work, and it is so different from just hearing. This short, humorous story reflects the ability to respond properly when we have true clarity of understanding. It also reflects the problems that can arise when we react as a result of poor listening skills and the impact others experience. Another application for this story is communication. Is the person to whom we are speaking properly interpreting and understanding the message we are sending? This would be an excellent story to interject into a class on listening skills or effective communication.

Three Key Applications

- Effectively Listening
- Having Clarity of Understanding
- Communicating Effectively

Everything is Just Fine!—The Story

A husband and wife are driving down the road. It is a beautiful, warm, sunny summer day. The lady spots an ice cream store down the road and would love to have an ice cream cone. She says to her husband, "Honey, would you like an ice cream cone?" Her husband quickly replies, "No thanks honey, I'm fine," and drives on. About five blocks later the husband looks over at his wife and notices that she looks rather upset. "Honey, is everything okay?" he asks. She responds in a rather negative tone, "Everything is just fine!"

Other Insights:

She really wanted that ice cream cone, but she did not deliver her message very well. Say what you mean, and mean what you say! Not only do we need to be good listeners, but we also must be effective communicators.

Not only do we need to be good listeners, but we also must be effective communicators.

He's My Friend—Applications

This story shows us the importance of looking beyond the surface, facing the reality of a situation, and accepting the truth. The old expression, "can't see the forest for the trees" applies—having the ability to look beyond the superficial and seeing people for who they really are.

Three Key Applications

- Looking Beyond the Obvious
- Not Being Quick to Judge
- Respecting

He's My Friend—The Story

When my son Adam (who is now twenty-five years old, married, a chemical engineer, and at this writing, a first lieutenant in the U.S. Army serving in Afghanistan) was in the third grade, he was very excited about a new friend he had made. Every day when Adam would return home from school, he would tell us about Derek. "He's my friend! Derek and I play together. We're buddies. We do everything together." Adam would go on and on about Derek, praising him and always stating proudly, "He's my friend."

An afternoon open house was coming up in a few weeks, which would involve students, teachers, and parents. Adam couldn't wait for us to meet his teacher, Mrs. Tackahashi. But, even more, he was so excited because we would finally be able to meet his friend, Derek. Actually, as a result of all that Adam had told us about Derek, we felt that we already knew him. We pictured a boy quite like our son—very active, very healthy, and full of energy and vitality. What other picture could we have formed with all the exploits Adam shared with us? "We do all sorts of things together," Adam would say. "He's my friend."

On the day of the open house, we were excited to visit Adam's school, talk with his teacher, and finally have the opportunity to meet his friend Derek. Mrs. Tackahashi beamed with enthusiasm about all the projects her third-grade students had displayed for the open house. Adam was pleased with his teacher's comments regarding him, and we were equally delighted that he was doing so well. After some planned activities, there was time to mingle and meet other faculty, parents, and students. Adam took us by the hand and moved us through the others exclaiming, "Derek is over here. I want you to meet my friend." Sitting by the window in a wheel chair was Derek. He had very short, deformed arms, and as we approached, he pushed himself from the chair and crawled toward us. His legs were useless. "Mom, Dad, this is Derek. He's my friend." We were momentarily stunned, but quickly recovered and greeted Derek. He was a bright young man, full of energy and vitality, just like Adam.

Later that evening at home, the three of us and Adam's sister, Diana, discussed the open house. "Isn't Derek neat? He's my best friend," Adam said. We looked at our son proudly. Adam possessed a quality so many of us often desire. He was able to look beyond the surface of a situation. He was able to see past Derek's infirmities and see the real person. He saw his friend.

We all agreed the open house was a great success and Derek was quite a young man. Adam was very fortunate to have Derek for a friend.

Other Insights:

Are there times when you only looked superficially at a situation, a task, and a person? What was the result? Different does not equal wrong. Different simply equals different. So often we can be quick to judge rather than to understand. Understanding so often leads to respect, and respect to appreciating and valuing. Take the time to look beyond the obvious; it can make all the difference in the world.

See people for who they really are. Take the time to look beyond the obvious.

Killer Statements— Applications

This story demonstrates the power of words and the impact they can have on others. It speaks strongly of respect for the dignity of every single person and treating others the way we ourselves would like to be treated.

Three Key Applications

- Respecting Others
- Using the Golden Rule
- Recognizing the Impact of Words

Killer Statements— The Story

A young college freshman was off to a very good beginning for his first year away from home—attending college and having the opportunity to play the sport he loved, football.

Now, this person was not a particularly handsome individual. He was very self-conscious of this fact and thought of himself with a variety of denigrating terms such as homely and even ugly. He had not dated during his high school years and had attended his senior prom with a group of friends from the high school football team. Despite this, he was not a sad individual. He enjoyed friendships and experienced success in both his academic and athletic involvement. However, he was always self-conscious and aware of his appearance.

His college team had started the season with a string of victories. They had four wins and no losses. He was a starter on the team, his studies were going well, and all seemed to be moving along in a positive direction. However, something was missing. The young man was hoping for a relationship, and as a result of his self-consciousness over his appearance, he faced quite a dilemma. "Why would anyone want to go out with me? I'm ugly. Why would any girl want to have a relationship with someone like me?" These concerns and thoughts were firmly embedded and impacted the young man's confidence. To make matters worse, there was a particular cheerleader who had caught his attention. He found himself very attracted to this young lady and thought of her frequently, even though he felt it was hopeless and futile to think anything would ever develop between the two of them.

On the evening of their fifth consecutive victory, the young man, after listening to his head coach's praises of the hard work they had done and the accomplishments that their hard work had led to, joined in the team celebrations. The team, coaches, cheerleaders, and support staff had all shared a fine dinner together. As he was about to call it an evening and head back over to his residence hall, he noticed the cheerleader he was so attracted to walking over to him. He was dumbfounded as she walked over and sat down next to him. "Hi, I was wondering if you would like to go out with me this Friday," said the young lady. The young man could not believe the words he had just heard coming from the very person who was the object of his affections. "That would be great!" he said to her smiling and thinking how fortunate he was. "That's wonderful!" exclaimed the girl as she went on to say, "You see the sorority I'm pledging for said I have to ask an ugly person out to the party for this Friday, and I thought of you right away." As the girl walked away, the young man sat there stunned. All his self-conscious thoughts had been confirmed in one brief, painful moment. He walked slowly back to his room, and there, when he was all alone, he cried.

Other Insights:

That young thoughtless lady never realized the pain she inflicted that evening. She had dated hundreds of times and for the most part felt that anyone given an opportunity to be with her was very lucky. She was doing this person a favor. Life went on as usual for her, completely oblivious to the feelings of others.

That young man on the other hand was crushed. He was taken down so low that it would literally take him years to recuperate. As a result of that one moment and that "killer statement" spoken to him, he did not date for the remainder of his college years.

We often hurt or injure others with our spoken words. We call these "killer statements." They are unnecessary, thoughtless words that cut to the quick. Remember the spoken word once spoken is very difficult to take back. The damage is done.

What killer statements have you used with others?

What impact did they have?

Your words have a significant impact on others. Don't deliver "killer statements."

PIG!—Applications

When people speak, do you hear opportunities or threats? This story relates to our perception, our own preconceived ideas, and the way we interpret incoming messages. It's a short, humorous story that will cause people to reflect on how they themselves react or respond to various situations they are confronted with.

Three Key Applications

- What are You Hearing?
- How are You Interpreting It?
- Using Appropriate Listening Skills

PIG!—The Story

A man is driving down a mountainous winding road in his sports car. It is a beautiful, sunny day. He has his convertible top down, and he's driving along enjoying the majesty of the environment. He sees another car approaching, and as it gets closer, he notices that a woman is driving and she has her head out of the window. As the two cars come closer, he slows down and hears the woman yell "PIG!" The man quickly reacts by yelling back, "COW!" The lady's car moves on up the winding road and the man continues on his way. As he picks up speed and goes around the next turn in the road, he runs right into a large pig.

When people yell, will you hear threats or opportunities?

Other Insights:

At times, our listening skills can really be challenged. An upset customer or a person using loud, inappropriate language or speaking with an accent can all put our listening skills to the test. This is when we truly need to be active listeners and work hard to achieve clarity of understanding. It's easy to simply react and raise our voices or join in with inappropriate remarks. Also, if our patience is being put to the test, we often simply withdraw. If you've ever been in such a situation, you know the result is usually a lose-lose for both you and the other person. This is where one's professionalism is really put to the test. It takes a great deal of energy to truly listen to what is being said and achieve understanding so that you can respond to the situation properly.

Do you use a *Ready–Fire–Aim* versus a *Ready–Aim–Fire* approach or do you use a *Situation–Respond–Evaluate* versus a *Situation–Evaluate–Respond* approach?

When people yell, will you hear threats or opportunities?

Get Her the Oranges!—Applications

This story is about caring, going the extra mile, and doing what is right, necessary, proper, and just when it is called for. It also may be applied to effective teamwork and the power of a common goal.

Three Key Applications

- Applying Teamwork
- Going Beyond the Call of Duty
- Caring

Get Her the Oranges!— The Story

At the age of eleven, I was a sole survivor of a very serious accident, which left me strapped into some traction the likes of which I could not have imagined. This was not going to be a fast healing process. A minimum of eighteen months of physical confinement lay ahead of me. I found out early on that it was much faster and easier to comply with the doctors, nurses, and other medical staff. It was also less painful. For this reason, I never asked for anything, but rather resigned myself to what was provided. At least once a day, a well-meaning member of the hospital staff would stop by to explain to me that if I needed or wanted anything, all I had to do was ask, but I never did. Then one night, months into my recovery, I wanted an orange. The night nurse came in to check on me and, as was standard, asked if I needed anything. She looked shocked when I announced my need for an orange.

That moment is where this story begins. The entire floor was summoned to search the lunch bags, refrigerators, etc., for an orange. After all, I had never asked for anything before, so this was an important request. No orange was found, but they did not give up. The security guard of the floor I was on (6th floor) contacted the security guard of the 5th floor, and the same frantic search began with the same results. The 4th floor was contacted and so on floor by floor until finally, after an exhausted search, the security guard in the emergency room was called. As life (and luck) would have it, this was the same guard who had been present when I was brought to the hospital following the accident. He remembered me well. Although he did not have an orange, and like the other guards could not leave his post, he did have a plan.

He called his sleeping wife, explained to her that the little girl he had told her about months before needed an orange, and there were none to be found. Well, that would not do. So his wife left her warm, and no doubt comfortable, bed to drive to an all-night grocery store. After purchasing a bag of oranges, she drove all the way to the hospital emergency room where her husband waited. He took the oranges to the 1st floor security guard who took them to the 2nd floor, who in turn took them to the 3rd and so on until they were delivered to my room by a beaming nurse and an equally happy security guard. The oranges were delicious!

Other Insights:

Months would pass before I would fully know the efforts that had been made on my behalf that night. Soon after, a security guard approached me, gently took my hand and asked, "Did you get your oranges?"

I had no idea why so many people would be willing to come together for such a simple request.

It has been 28 years since that simple act of kindness, and I have never forgotten those oranges nor any of the people who went well beyond the call of duty that night to meet the request of one little girl. That night, they brought me more than oranges. They brought me some life lessons to learn.

You see, going beyond the call of duty matters, and small gestures aren't small to the recipient. Teamwork does create value, and a team can be spontaneously developed when a common goal presents itself. These lessons are part of my life, both personally and professionally. And, they began as a desire for an orange.

Story by ***Julie Poto***

Going beyond the call of duty matters, and small gestures aren't small to the recipient.

The Cook, the Carpenter, and the Engineer— Applications

This story relates to knowing when to leave well enough alone and let it be. Sometimes we need to go with the flow, observe a situation, and recognize when opportunities are presenting themselves to us. This story may apply to selling (knowing when to stop talking and not oversell), effective communication, and the power of perception.

Three Key Applications

- Using Passive Communication
- Understanding with Two-Way Communication
- Knowing When to Listen

The Cook, the Carpenter, and the Engineer— The Story

During the French Revolution, there were many who, as a result of their political beliefs and the side they chose to support, were unfortunately sent to the guillotine—that infamous killing device used for beheading people. On one particular day, there were three individuals who were scheduled for executions; a cook, a carpenter, and an engineer were brought out before the crowd and momentarily placed on display as their fate was readied.

The cook was brought up first and positioned on the guillotine. His head lay beneath the huge blade and he awaited his inevitable future. When the lever was pulled, nothing happened, as the blade remained suspended high above. The crowd took this as an act of God and demanded that the cook be released unharmed and set free. It was so ordered by those in charge overseeing the events of the day. The cook was released from the restraints that bound him and set free. He quickly ran down the stairs and disappeared into the crowd.

Next, the carpenter was brought up, positioned, and the lever was pulled— once again, nothing. The huge blade gleamed high above in the sun. Now, the guillotine had been thoroughly checked and tested that morning as it was every morning, and those in attendance knew this. Again, the crowd roared for the release of the condemned man. Those in charge yielded, fearing a riot and believing that a higher authority might be speaking out in judgment. They ordered the carpenter released in addition to the cook and, desiring to move things along quickly, focused their attention on the third individual, the engineer.

The engineer was led up the stairs to the guillotine. Now, he had a keen eye for detail and had been observing the workings of the guillotine. He felt he had a true understanding of how this huge mechanism worked. As the engineer was escorted to the top of the stairs, he turned to face those in charge— his executioners—and stated, "You know, I can fix this thing and get it working properly if you will just untie my hands and give me a few minutes."

Other Insights:

Know when to be quiet and listen. Know when to ask questions and achieve clarity of understanding.

Have you ever spoken up at the wrong or inappropriate moment? What was the result? We need to realize that there are times when passive communication is called for and there are times when we need to incorporate two-way active communication to promote understanding.

Have you ever oversold when your customer had already decided to buy only to change his mind as a result of your continued persistence? Know when to back off and be quiet.

Know when to be quiet and listen. Only then can we truly understand the significance of a situation.

Pandora's Box Revisited—Applications

This is a story dealing with trust, something that can take years to build and only seconds to destroy. This story applies to building relationships and establishing a firm, sound, strong starting point upon which to build a future with a customer or another person.

Three Key Applications

- Establishing Relationships
- Retaining Relationships
- Building Trust

Pandora's Box Revisited— The Story

A salesperson had an important meeting with the top executive of an organization. He had been attempting to get this appointment for many months, and he was thrilled with the potential sales that such a meeting might produce. Upon his arrival, he was greeted by the CEO's assistant and led to his office. The executive greeted him and said, "I'm so glad you're here. I look forward to our meeting. However, please excuse me for a brief moment. Something has come up that requires my attention. Please make yourself comfortable here in my office. Feel free to look around (the office was quite spacious and beautifully decorated) and examine any of the items here. Just please do not touch the box on the center of my desk." And, with those words, the executive departed.

The salesperson felt quite pleased to be there and, taking off his coat, made himself comfortable. He scanned his surroundings and found the office to be one of the most lavish he had ever been in. He again thought about his good fortune to have this meeting and all that might happen as a result of building this relationship. As he gazed around the room at the beautiful paintings and rather extravagant decorations, his attention could not help but be brought to the item resting in the middle of the large desk. It was the one item the CEO had specifically mentioned not to touch. What could it possibly be, thought the salesperson? It's just a plain rectangular box about 15 inches long sitting right there in the middle of his desk. Oh well, I'll just look at these other items. He walked around the room observing the many varied items displayed in the CEO's office. He could not, however, stop thinking about the executive's words as he left... *"Examine any of the items here. Just please do not touch the box on the center of my desk."*

The salesperson tried to focus elsewhere, but could not help being drawn time and time again to the black box in the middle of the large desk. As his curiosity grew, he moved closer to the desk and, walking around it, observed each side of the black box. What could it possibly be? What could be so important about that silly little box? Why should I not be allowed to touch it?

The salesperson walked back over to the office door and, opening it, checked down the hall. No one could be seen. He closed the door and went back over by the desk. His curiosity had now overwhelmed him with an incredible sense of urgency to know why he should not be able, not be allowed, to touch the black box.

He leaned over the desk and reaching out ever so gently touched the box. That's all it took! The box had apparently been filled with small BB-like bearings, thousands of them, and they quickly began to pour out all over the desk, onto the floor, and spread throughout the room. The salesperson let out a shriek, grabbed the box, fell to his knees, and began attempting to pick up the tiny bearings and refill the box. It was precisely at that moment when the office door opened and the CEO returned. He looked at the salesperson now down on his hands and knees desperately trying to return things to their original state. He asked the salesperson to please stop what he was doing and stand. He then went on to say, "Unfortunately, our meeting is over. You cannot be trusted!" The salesperson was quickly escorted from the building and all hope of building a relationship with this company was now gone.

Other Insights:

When we lose trust, we lose everything. We need to create service, not servicecide. How do you build and retain trust with your customers? It is such a precious commodity upon which your relationship rests. Protect it and preserve it!

Trust is so fragile. It can take years to build and only seconds to destroy.

You Can't Put It Back—Applications

This story applies to treating customers the way they want to be treated—delivering service, solving problems, and responding to their needs. This story fits in particularly well with any customer service training program emphasizing quality service and no excuses.

Three Key Applications

- Delivering Excellent Customer Service
- Responding to Customer Needs
- Eliminating Excuses

You Can't Put It Back— The Story

Take a tube of toothpaste and try this little experiment. For each customer excuse you have given for not delivering excellent service, squeeze out an amount of toothpaste equal to what you would use to brush your teeth. Ten excuses equals ten squeezes, fifteen equals fifteen squeezes, and so forth. After you have recalled those excuses and have squeezed out the appropriate amount of toothpaste, try the following. Put it back! That's right, push it in, squeeze it in, whatever you must do, put it back! It's not very easy is it? Most give up after a short period of time, realizing they really can't put it back without resorting to extraordinary measures.

When you give excuses for your service or rather lack of it, just remember that the spoken word once spoken is very difficult to take back and repair. Just like that tube of toothpaste, it's never quite the same again. It can be a real challenge and often impossible to regain the trust and confidence you have lost with a particular customer as a result of the excuses you allowed to slip out.

Other Insights:

Deliver the service you know that you would desire if you were the customer. Deliver the service you know you are capable of presenting to your customer. Deliver excellent customer service and build a customer-responsive relationship to keep the customer coming back time and time again, knowing they will not be getting excuses, but rather what they want—**service**!

There should be no excuses for not delivering excellent customer service.

Where are You Going?— Applications

Just as a ship must have a course to properly plot out its journey, arrive at each port of call on schedule, and proceed on its way at the appropriate time, always focused on its direction and "the big picture," so too must we.

This story relates to vision, mission, strategic objectives, sense of direction, core competencies, and core values, which must all support and complement the identified direction whether relating to an individual's concerns, a team, a department, a division, or an entire organization. We need to know where we are going and have a sense of direction.

Three Key Applications

- Charting Your Course
- Defining Your Vision and Mission
- Looking at the "Big Picture"

Where are You Going?— The Story

Remember the story of Alice in Wonderland where Alice is wandering down that road that is taking her on her journey? She comes to an area where the road divides and goes off in two directions. "I don't know which road to take," says Alice. "Where are you going?" asked the Cheshire cat in the tree nearby. Alice responds, "I don't really know." "Then it doesn't matter which road you take," says the Cheshire cat. "It will take you there."

Back in the 1960s, there was a poster that said, "Chances are that if you don't know where you are going, you're probably going to end up someplace else and don't be surprised when you get there." Each of us needs to have our own personal compass—our sense of direction as to where we are going and how we are going to get there.

Other Insights:

Where are you going as an individual, or as the member of a team or a company?

We need to have an identified direction. One does not usually plan a trip without a destination, a planned itinerary, or a map to make certain we make the best use of our time. Our life's journey needs similar attention to enhance our chances of a safe, meaningful, and joyful trip.

What is your vision? Where do you want to be in the next five to eight years? What is your mission? Usually, this encompasses a two-to-four-year period of time. Finally, what are your yearly goals? These should all be in alignment with each other or they can produce such things as confusion, chaos, catastrophe, and a sense of being lost. When your goals support your mission, which in turn complement and support your vision, you have successfully charted your course.

Chances are that if you don't know where you're going, you're probably going to end up someplace else and don't be surprised when you get there.

The Game—Applications

This story reflects team focus, concern, and success—not just focusing on self, but the entire group. This reflects the commitment required to properly move from an "I" focus to a "We" focus when one has accepted the responsibility of being a team member.

Three Key Applications

- Having a Team Focus
- Going from "I" to "We"
- Going from Independent to Interdependent

The Game—The Story

A mother was preparing lunch one afternoon when her two boys came running into the house from their morning baseball game. They both played on the same team, and as they came into the kitchen, their mother greeted them. She turned to the first boy as he came in and asked, "How was the game?" "It was great," he said. "I got a home run and a double." "That's wonderful," said his mom. She turned to her other son as he followed in. "How was the game?" she repeated the question to her other child. "Oh, it wasn't so good, we lost," he said.

Other Insights:

It takes a fully functional independent "I" to be a member of a fully functional interdependent "We." Once you make that commitment to be a team member, that transition requires a new focus—moving from "I" to "We"—realizing that it is no longer "as I succeed, I am fulfilled," but as "we succeed, I am fulfilled."

It takes a fully functional independent "I" to be a member of a fully functional interdependent "We."

The Teachers' Lounge—Applications

The impact of maintaining a positive attitude and the destructiveness of a negative attitude are what this story is all about. Attitude is such a powerful force in our lives. It literally permeates everything we do. It is your choice what impact your attitude will have on others. Do you choose to be uplifting and spread cheer, or do you choose to be negative and spread doom and gloom?

Three Key Applications

- Creating a Positive Attitude
- Having a Pleasant Greeting
- Having a Significant Impact

The Teachers' Lounge—
The Story

A young, enthusiastic high school teacher was having a great day. As he walked toward the faculty lounge, he couldn't help but think about how good his morning had been. The students were really involved and their participation was exceptional. He felt like he was making a difference and looked forward to his afternoon classes with equal anticipation.

Walking into the faculty lounge, he removed his lunch from the refrigerator and grabbed an available chair across from two other familiar teachers. These two teachers seemed to always be in the faculty lounge. There were times when the young teacher wondered what it was they did. These two were always griping and complaining about something. It was Monday or it was Wednesday, or it was morning or evening, or it was too hot or too cold. They might be putting down a colleague or a student. No matter what, nothing was ever right, and they always had something to complain about. And, you know, that negativity can spread like a cancer. It can bring others down as well.

The young teacher quickly finished his lunch and upon leaving the faculty lounge was thinking, "Why did I go in there? I feel terrible. It's going to take a lot of energy to get back to the way I was feeling prior to sitting down to lunch with those two."

Other Insights:

You own your attitude. The attitude you bring to work with you each day truly has an impact on not only yourself, but on those you come into contact with. Did you wake up this morning and say, "Good morning, God" or "Good God it's morning"? Your attitude permeates everything you do and has a significant impact on the way you face each day.

Your attitude permeates everything you do and has a significant impact on the way you face each day.

What is Your Story?— Applications

Each one of us has at least one meaningful, uplifting story to tell—something that personally happened to us or something we observed or heard. These stories need to be told. They need desperately to be heard. Your story keeps alive "what is right" for others to live and learn from. Your story contributes to the corporate culture of your place of business. It builds a realistic path for others to follow and imitate. It reflects behaviors that touch the heart and encourage like behavior. The stories act as a compass, a guideline, a directional beacon as to which way to go, not only within your place of work, but within a place of worship, an educational facility, a home, or a family.

We encourage you to not only tell your story, but to encourage others to tell and share theirs. Building a collection of these stories can lend significant support to the way of life (culture) being nurtured within your organization. As you build a collection of stories, you will discover that you have gathered a powerful set of instructional tools that reveals the heart of your company.

Three Key Applications

- Creating Stories About Your Company Culture
- Developing "What is Right"
- Building a Path for Others to Follow

Building Your Story

Here are some thoughts, insights, and guidelines for you to use as you construct your stories and put the values of your culture into print.

Your story should have a beginning, a middle, and an end. Something that happened to you personally is a great place to get started. It doesn't have to be anything grandiose. Sometimes the simplest story can pack the largest wallop for the appropriate moment and setting (see the story "My Best Friend"). Your story should have a moral or lesson to impart—a positive, meaningful message for others to reflect on, imitate, or use as an example of "what is right." Use dates, names, and specific instances whenever and wherever possible. These add to the credibility and acceptance of your story. Tell about something you have a passion for or something that had a significant impact on you. When you talk from the heart, it is difficult not to be received well. When you touch other hearts, it is difficult not to be remembered.

The story should reflect how you felt at the time of its occurrence. On average, telling your story should take between two and six minutes. It should be about an event or an activity that reflects positive values. Remember that you want to nurture appropriate behavior and values. Even though we stated that a personal experience is often best, it can be something heard or shared by another. If the story celebrates a victory of sorts for your company or a core value, or complements the organization's vision, you're on the right track. Remember that this is a teaching tool. Ask yourself, what do I want to teach? What message do I want to convey to others as a result of this experience? We also highly recommend that your personal stories along with others be collected and saved. They reflect the collective values of your organization and provide a powerful learning tool.

Your story will be remembered, passed on to others, shared, and will lend to the creation of other stories in the future. It is a building block of tradition, values, and the individuals who have made your company, school, church, family, etc., what it is today and points the direction to where it is going tomorrow. Give your story the sincere thought it deserves and title it appropriately. It's your story! Only you can tell it! Only you can put it down in writing in your own unique way and share it with others. Have fun!

When you talk from the heart, it is difficult not to be received well. When you touch other hearts, it is difficult not to be remembered.

Your story desperately needs to be heard—tell it!

Authors' Personal Information

Rose D. Sloat and Darryl S. Doane are managing partners of The Learning Service, Ltd. They are international performance-based training and development specialists. They focus on customer service, sales training, leadership/managerial skills development, effectively dealing with change and transition, the critical role of attitude in one's life, and long-term performance improvement.

They are co-authors of the *Customer Service Activities Book*. Their other published works include *The New Sales Game* and *The New Sales Game Participant's Book*, a program focusing on the outside sales force and the quest to move from service to solutions providers. They are also co-authors of the book, *EXCUSES, EXCUSES, EXCUSES...For Not Delivering Excellent Customer Service—And What Should Happen!* In addition, they are the co-authors and editors of 50 *Activities for Achieving Excellent Customer Service*.

Darryl S. Doane

Darryl has served as a teacher, speaker, facilitator, and professional consultant for over 30 years. He has presented outstanding programs to numerous individuals including adult, college, and youth organizations, churches, civic groups, and corporate America. He has worked with national organizations such as the National Association of Student Councils and Secondary Schools Principals and was a participant in NASA's Teacher in Space Program. He served as Senior Training Specialist for a billion-dollar corporation for seven years prior to becoming a managing partner and co-creator of The Learning Service, Ltd.

Rose D. Sloat

Rose served as the training coordinator of a billion-dollar company for 15 years. Rose is an outstanding facilitator who has learned, taught, and applied every component within the training arena from organizing and scheduling training to writing and producing learning events. Rose has enabled The

Learning Service, Ltd., to become an effective and efficient means of quality learning for companies that have chosen to outsource their training needs. She serves on the board of a support group for women (WIN—Women's Initiative) in the capacity of president. She also is currently an officer of a local Toastmasters Club #3342 and holds the position of vice president of Education. Rose is a managing partner and co-creator of The Learning Service, Ltd.